Lord, Sometimes I Don't Feel Saved!

C. Michael Moss

Lord, Sometimes I Don't Feel Saved!

Renewing
Our
Confidence
In
Christ

COVENANT
PUBLISHING

All Scripture quotations, unless otherwise indicated, are the author's own translations from the original New Testament Greek text.

Scripture quotations marked NIV are taken from the HOLY BIBLE: NEW INTERNATIONAL VERSION®. NIV®. Copyright © 1973, 1978, 1984 by International Bible Society. Used by permission of Zondervan Publishing House. All rights reserved.

www.covenantpublishing.com

P.O. Box 390 · Webb City, Missouri 64870
Call toll free at 877.673.1015

Library of Congress Cataloging-in-Publication Data

Moss, C. Michael (Carl Michael), 1950-
  Lord, sometimes I don't feel saved! : renewing our confidence in Christ / C. Michael Moss.
     p. cm.
  Includes bibliographical references.
  ISBN 1-892435-20-9 (pbk.)
  1. Bible. N.T. Epistles of John—Commentaries. I. Title.
  BS2805.53 .M67 2002
  227'.94077—dc21

                              2002003363

Dedication

Dedicated to Ginny, Becky, Abby, and Carrie—
My wife and my daughters,
The ladies in my life who have loved, encouraged, and understood.

Acknowledgments

This book has grown out of several lectures at local churches and classes at Lipscomb University; each time I have led in a study of 1 John I have been enriched. I owe my gratitude to listeners who have helped me to rethink John's message.

I am also grateful to the numerous students who asked to read as I wrote and who encouraged me to persevere. Their interest is of special importance to me because I will always see myself not as a writer but as a teacher. Special thanks are also due to all who has served as volunteer proofreaders, checked my style, made helpful suggestions about sections that lacked clarity, and helped me write so my prospective audience could understand what I wanted to say.

When we thank those who contributed most to an effort, the one who deserves the highest accolades may well be the one who put up with the most. Love and thanks go to my wife and daughters who heard various lessons from 1 John in multiple settings. To my daughters who complained little and to my wife who complained not at all, I appreciate your understanding.

Table of Contents

Introduction

> *Now faith is being sure of what we hope for
> and certain of what we do not see.*
>
> Hebrews 11:1

"Lord, sometimes I don't feel saved!" Have you ever found yourself in that dilemma? The harsh reality of the human circumstance forces us Christians to face our own failings and inadequacy before God. For Christians to grow as God's people, they must be conscious that they *can fall* and, at the same time, *feel secure* in their relationship with God. Walking that tightrope will never be easy!

Jack Exum described an experience that illustrates that dilemma. While holding a meeting in a small town in Ohio, he went to the little restaurant next door to the motel where he was staying. The proprietor of the motel assumed that, since he was a preacher, he was bound to have a great deal in common with a minister from one of the denominations in the town. So he introduced the two men. Jack, who is known for his candor, began the discussion by saying, "Oh yes, you are from a denomination that teaches once saved always saved." "Yes, that's right," replied the minister. "No, that's wrong," retorted Jack. Not to be out done, the minister said, "I assume then that you are from a religious body that teaches 'never really sure you're saved.'" After considerable thought, Jack reluctantly responded, "Yes, I suppose that's right." Back came the rejoinder, "No, that's wrong."

Praise the Lord that salvation does not rest on my accomplisments but upon God's work in Jesus!

Over 2,000 years ago, Aristotle said, "Perfection is the golden mean." The difficulty is that the pendulum has a tendency to swing from one extreme to the other. In correcting one problem, we often create another (see Figure 1). The perspective of the Bible is not "once saved always saved," or how does one explain the warnings of the letters regarding the possibility of apostasy (cf., Romans 6:1-14; 1 Corinthians 10:1-13; Hebrews 6:1-12)? We can never grow cocky about our status. To do so would make us slothful about service. Grace and God's protection can never mean license. Likewise, our perspective should not be "never really sure I'm saved" (cf., 1 John 5:13). Many Christians respond to the question "Are you saved?" with "I hope so," "If I don't commit some terrible sin," "I guess I won't know until the judgment day," or "I don't know." Is it any wonder that with such an attitude one would have difficulty living the Christian life with excitement and zeal? *Praise the Lord that salvation does not rest on my accomplishments but upon God's work in Jesus!*

The apostle John was writing to first-century Christians who were facing the same problem. Something or someone was producing a lack of confidence regarding their salvation. John, near the end of his first letter, tells his readers, "I have written these things to you, who believe in the name of the Son of God, in order that you might know that you have eternal life" (1 John 5:13). John has given his audience benchmarks by which they can examine their lives and thus their relationship with God.

Martin Luther is said to have met his servant early one morning. The servant asked, "Master, do you feel like a child of God today?" Luther replied, "No, I can't say that I do, but I know that I am." That is where the Christian should be able to take a stand.

Our procedure will be first to set each of John's letters in its historical context. The first step in good exegesis (explaining what a text means) is to determine the intended message for its original audience. Next we will apply that message to our situation today. We should never begin with "What does it say to me?" Such an approach can lead to a subjective reading of the message that will miss both God's message for the original audience and His message for His church today. The Bible was not written to me in the twenty-first century, but it has been preserved for me and is God's Word to me. I must discover God's message for those first readers and then apply His message to my life.

A "Personal Inventory" appears at the conclusion of each chapter. The inventory and following discussion questions, "Let's Get Personal," have been gleaned from John's letters. These questions are designed to assist us in examining our relationship with God. Hopefully the inventory will provide objective standards that will enable Christians to feel secure in that relationship even though they will still sometimes say, "Lord, sometimes I don't feel saved!"

Figure 1

The Pendulum Swings

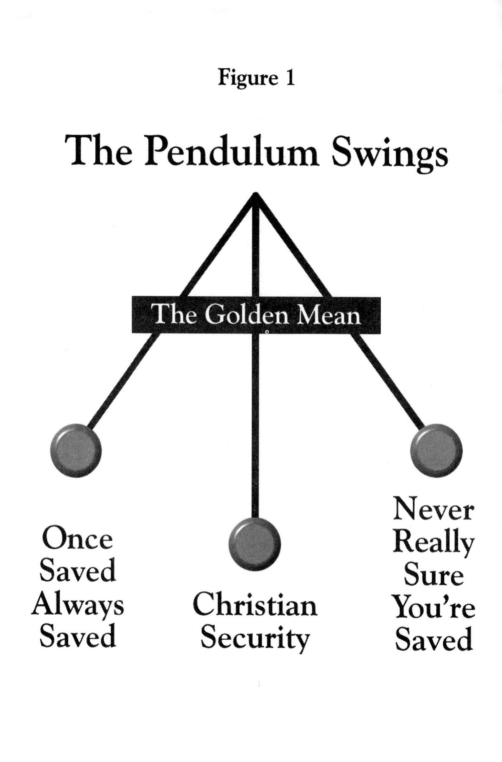

The Golden Mean

Once
Saved
Always
Saved

Christian
Security

Never
Really
Sure
You're
Saved

Chapter 1

Identifying the Bad Guys

By their fruit you will recognize them.
Matthew 7:16

In classic TV Westerns, it was always easy to tell the bad guys from the good guys. The bad guys would always wear black hats and do despicable things. In the real world things are not that easy to tell apart. Undoubtedly those who were producing the insecurity in the lives of John's audience seemed to be enlightened, sincere Christians. They did not wear black hats. They did not intend to be mean and despicable, nor did they intend purposefully to teach falsehood. If we are to understand John's letters, it is essential to know something about these opponents and their teaching.

The Security Robbers: Gnosticism and Doceticism

Two keys words, *Gnosticism and Doceticism*, describe the opponents of John who were robbing the Christians of their security.

Gnosticism

The term, Gnosticism, comes from the Greek word for "knowledge."[1] Although full-fledged Gnosticism would not develop until the second century, already this attempt to wed Platonism (a philosophy that began with Plato's sharp distinction between matter and spirit) and Christianity was beginning to exert its influence upon the church. Members of the group held that they possessed a *special* knowledge that was deeper and more genuine than that held by ordinary Christians. We can see how this religious snobbery could produce a sense of inferiority and insecurity on the part of those "ordinary Christians." These proto-gnostics were dualists, holding that matter was bad and spirit was good. Thus a *good* god could not be closely associated with the *created* world. A lower deity, the God of the Old Testament or the Demiurge, had to be credited with creating the world. *Sin* for them was ignorance of the human condition and the nature of the universe. It was not a matter of *wrongdoing*. When the Gnostic was baptized, he was resurrected and became "otherworldly." On account of this, bodily resurrection was denied, and sin (or wrongdoing) was a matter of indifference. Strangely enough, a single group could be both ascetic (denying the body all types of pleasures) and hedonistic (engaging in sensuous excesses). For them, the body was matter and thus bad. You could commit an act and claim that, although your body did the act, your mind was somehow uninvolved.

Docetism

The second term, *Doceticism*, is also used to describe the view members of this movement held regarding the nature of Christ. Docetic teachers claimed that Jesus only "seemed"[2] to suffer. Again, a good god would need to be separated from evil matter. He could never really take on *flesh*. He could never suffer. From the primary good God emanated or flowed other lesser gods. Among these emanations were Christ and/or *Logos* (the Greek word for "Word") and/or *Monogenes* (the Greek word for "only begotten"). The man Jesus was simply a ghost or a good man whose body the Christ used when the good God adopted Him.

Papias, Polycarp, Irenaeus, and Hippolytus tell stories about John, the disciple of the Lord, and an early second-century false teacher, Cerinthus, whose teaching John refuted. Whether you accept these accounts as reliable or not, the following summary of their accounts does provide a picture of the teaching which John sought to refute:

> Cerinthus was educated in the wisdom of the Egyptians. He taught that the world was not created by the primary God but by a power separated from him and ignorant of him. Cerinthus taught that Jesus had not been born of a virgin, but was simply a son of Joseph and Mary. He was, however, wiser and more righteous than other men. Christ descended upon Jesus in the form of a dove. He then proclaimed the unknown Father and performed miracles. Christ departed from Jesus leaving him alone. Jesus then rose again. John refuted Cerinthus' teaching of knowledge falsely so-called.

As early as AD 110 (twenty years or less after John penned his letters), Ignatius, in his letter to the church at Smyrna, responded to a similar heresy. He argued that Jesus was truly born of a virgin and baptized by John. He was really nailed on a cross, really suffered, and was really raised from the dead.

The aim of these false teachers was not to profane the truths of the gospel. They wanted to clarify the message to make it both acceptable and attractive to the prevalent worldview. They were not ignorant. In fact, they would likely have possessed an above average IQ. They claimed that they had come to know the "mystery of the universe." In so doing they were above sin. Their claim of enlightenment, however, made "ordinary Christians" feel inferior. These believers did not know the special mystery; they saw shortcomings in their lives, namely their sins. Perhaps they were not good enough to receive the blessings of God. The joy of Christian living was beyond their reach.

Today's "Bad Guys"

Similar problems arise for Christians today. Those who bring insecurity today are not wearing black hats either. They do not intend to hurt anyone. They, like the Gnostics, come from within the "Christian circle." They as well seem to be sincere, enlightened Christians. The movements of which these people are a part began as correctives to real shortcomings within the church. Nevertheless, those who bring insecurity today share a common element with the heresy that John was combating. This fatal flaw is a misplaced emphasis—an emphasis that does not fall on the saving work of God in Jesus.

Liberalism

"Liberalism" is not a movement that originated out of a desire to destroy the security of the Christian. Its aim was to reexamine the Christian religion to see if superstition had crept into the faith of believers, to make Christianity acceptable to the modern mind. Critics from this movement, because of some presuppositions regarding the unacceptability of miracles to the modern mind, came to the conclusion that miracles, prophecies, and an errorless Bible inspired by God are the products of a Christian community which was naive, pre-scientific, and superstitious. Such a claim portrays the believer as naive, unthinking, and superstitious. Jesus becomes merely a good example, a good man, and a good teacher. The Christian religion becomes an anemic, be-a-good-person quest.

Health and Wealth Gospel

The "Health and Wealth" gospel often proclaimed over the airways today preaches a message that God will always bless His people with financial success. If they are His and heed His Word, these blessings are inevitable. He will provide healing for any illness if you truly believe. Struggling Christians that give generously and diligently strive to serve the Lord. Yet they are made to feel something is missing in their relationship with the Lord. They are not always healthy. Their finances may turn sour. God does care about the Christian's financial and physical welfare, and He is at work in the world; however, in the real world, many faithful Christians suffer due to a fallen creation. God has never healed every ailing Christian who trusts in Him. There has never been a time when every faithful believer was rich.

18

Charismatic Movement

The "Charismatic Movement" can likewise rob the "ordinary Christian" of security. This "ordinary Christian" does not possess the gifts, in particular the gift of tongues, and is, therefore, inferior to the "enlightened." The Charismatic Movement is itself another mystery, not the mystery of *Gnosis*, but a mystery all the same. The charismatic claims that the spiritual gifts are a sign that the Spirit is in the life of the Christian, a sign of spiritual maturity, a sign that you are saved. These claims fly in the face of the teaching of Paul in 1 Corinthians 12-14 that the quest for gifts is a sign of an *immature* church and not of maturity, that the Spirit gives the gifts as *He* deems best, and that tongues must be ranked as the *least* of the gifts. Yes, the Spirit is at work within Christians today. The issue is *how* He works.

Hyper Evangelism and Discipleship

Certain evangelistic or discipling efforts that emphasize special techniques and seek to govern every element in the Christian's life similarly can also produce a sense of inferiority. The group leader needs but six hours of sleep, knocks on fifty doors to witness each week, divulges his innermost thoughts to a special confessor, and has his special quiet time. To do less would mean that you are not a true disciple. The proponents of this movement are sincere and zealous. They are deeply committed to sharing the gospel with their neighbors. Yet a movement that will lead a young mother to come down the aisle at a worship assembly to confess her failings as a disciple when she is unable to give sufficient time to witnessing due to her three-month-old baby daughter exhibits faulty theology. Being a Christian mother is no less a part of the Christian calling than "door-knocking for the Lord." That is not to say that Christians ought not to be doing more to evangelize the world. It does point to the need for a full-orbed view of Christianity that encompasses all of our life and recognizes what God has accomplished in Jesus.

Wesleyanism

In the same way, "Wesleyanism" and its doctrines of *sinless* perfection and perfect love have often led the "ordinary Christian" to despair. Some reach despair when they do not receive the second work of grace, the special indwelling of the Spirit that enables you to reach a level beyond sin characterized by perfect love. The young woman, who feels she has "prayed through" on Sunday evening and then on Monday sins, is ready to give up. The young man who goes down the aisle at every "altar call" to "pray through" and never experiences this special measure of the Spirit feels inadequate and determines the Lord has no place for him. Often the very passages used to support such a system come from 1 John and rest on a misunderstanding of the background of the book. We do need to move toward deeper relationship with God. How, though, is that accomplished?

Legalism

"Legalism" calls Christians to find security in perfect obedience to a system of law. We must take seriously the commandments of God. But no one ever attains perfect obedience. We cannot question the zeal and sincerity of the adherents of such a system. That, however, does not help the feeling of inadequacy and failure that accompany living by such a system. Thank God that salvation and security do not depend on my own accomplishments! Well-meaning ministers, who sincerely want to lead their congregations to the worship pattern of the New Testament and to obedience to the commandments of God, have tacitly produced a salvation-by-works mentality. Any law-keeping system as the means of salvation minimizes, indeed blasphemes, the saving power of the blood of Christ. The apostle Paul called the Christians at Rome to realize that salvation has never been on the basis of human accomplishments! Salvation is by grace through faith. It always has been and always will be. Yes works will come,

My security must be found in my appropriation of the work of God in Jesus.

20

but they are never meritorious. In fact, you cannot have faith that does not act. *My security must be found in my appropriation of the work of God in Jesus.*

Is 1 John Really a Letter?

Understanding the nature of the "bad guys" in 1 John is important for a proper understanding of the book. It is also important to understand something of the nature of the book. Just what is this "letter" by John? Is it a letter? How should we characterize this brief book?

In the first century a letter normally followed a set pattern. First, the author introduced himself, for example, Paul, an apostle; or Sam, your tent maker. Next came recognition of the audience, for example, to the church at Philippi; or to my beloved daughter, Mary. A greeting and prayer would follow this. If the author were an adherent of Zeus, the greeting might be "rejoice" followed by "May Zeus grant you prosperity." For the Christian, the greeting might be "Grace to you and peace" followed by "May God the Father of the Lord Jesus fulfill your joy." After this would come the body of the letter. Finally, the author would close with a farewell.

A quick perusal of 1 John indicates that this book bears a few of the characteristics of a letter. First John begins with a classical prologue, much like Luke, John, and Hebrews. There is no indication of author or audience, no greeting, no prayer, and no final farewell. The book simply ends with the admonition "Little children, guard yourselves from idols."

In many ways this book bears the qualities we would expect to find in a "religious tract" today. It provides words of encouragement, teaching to refute heresy, and confirmation of the essence of the Christian faith.

The apostle John recognized a genuine need for this security on the part of his audience. The topic is no less relevant today. At some time, or perhaps even many times, in our pilgrimage, each of us has said, "Lord, sometimes I don't feel saved!"

PERSONAL INVENTORY

How am I handling the bad guys?

LET'S GET PERSONAL

1. What is the effect of labeling all false teachers as evil villains out to destroy the church? In so doing how do we tend to see modern day "bad guys" and people with good intentions?

2. What are the circumstances that lead to a sense of insecurity and inferiority for today's Christians?

3. Discuss the similarities between the "bad guys" in 1 John (the Gnostics and Docetics) and the modern day "bad guys" discussed in this chapter.

4. Respond to the following statement: "You are not a real Christian unless you are actively involved in evangelism."

5. Not all "bad guys" arise from within the "Christian circle." Discuss some other "bad guys" who arise out of the culture today.

6. Suppose someone were to ask you, "Are you saved?" How would you respond and why?

Chapter 2

Spiritual Russian Roulette

1 John 1:1-10

*What good is it for a man to gain
the whole world, yet forfeit his soul?*
Mark 8:36

Everyone is familiar with the deadly game called Russian roulette. Someone toying with life simply puts one bullet in the cylinder of a gun and spins the cylinder. He then puts the gun to his head and pulls the trigger. He has a one in six chance that the bullet will be in the chamber behind the hammer. He never knows for sure where that bullet is or what will be the outcome when he pulls the trigger. That is the way many view their Christian life. It is no more than a calculated gamble.

I came to grips with this idea as a junior in college. While home from school, college students at my home congregation would conduct devotionals at the homes of shut-ins. When it fell my lot to lead the devotional, we were discussing Christian security. The good sister in whose home we were meeting said, "If I were to back out of my driveway and someone were to crash into my car, and if I were to curse that person or think some terrible thought before being killed, I am convinced I would go straight to Hell!" The more I thought about her statement the more it bothered me. Oh, what a miserable situation! A Christian would always be just one sin, one slip, one mistake away from eternal damnation. The Christian life would be a spiritual Russian roulette.

Think for a moment about a sheet of paper with a line down the middle with one side labeled "lost" and the other "saved" (see Figure 2). The person who does not accept the saving work of God in Christ does not enjoy the promise of salvation. He or she is lost. Upon becoming a Christian, that person moves to the saved side of that ledger. Spiritual Russian roulette would then opt for the following plight: The first time I sin, I move to the lost side of the ledger. I penitently ask God for forgiveness, and He graciously forgives me. Again I am on the saved side of the ledger. It is not long before again I fail to live up to God's rules for me, and I sin. Again I move to the lost side. I ask God for forgiveness, and I am back on the saved side. And so it goes all my life—saved, lost, saved, lost, saved—back and forth, back and forth. The best I can do is to hope that I die on the right side of that imaginary line, to hope that there is no bullet in the chamber behind the hammer. Is it any wonder that, when the Christian life is viewed in this way, there is no sense of security? In chapter one of 1 John, John addresses this issue and sets the stage for a solution that he offers throughout the remainder of the book.

The Prologue[3]

1 John 1:1-4

[1:1]That which was from the beginning, that which we have heard, that which we have seen with our eyes, that which we have beheld and with our hands have handled, concerning the Word [*Logos*] of life [2](indeed this life was revealed, and we have seen and bear witness and proclaim to you the eternal life which was with the Father and was revealed to us), [3]that which we have seen and heard, we proclaim to you. We do this in order that you might have fellowship with us. Now our fellowship is with the Father and with His son Jesus Christ. [4]These things we are writing to you in order that our joy might be fulfilled.

John begins his letter with a classical introduction, a prologue. Chapter one verses one through three compose *one* complex sentence in the original Greek text! John alters the normal subject-verb-object word order to place special emphasis on the object—what was seen, heard, beheld, and touched. This one, the "Word of Life," the *Logos*, was no phantom. The Logos is not to be considered one distinct entity while the one who was heard, seen, and touched was another. Jesus is the Logos made flesh! "Seen," "heard," "beheld," and "handled" do not simply represent an event that occurred in the past. Instead of using a simple past tense in Greek, John used the perfect tense to emphasize the *abiding consequence of a past event*. John tells his audience, "This one is the one whom we have seen—we saw Him then, but that makes a difference now. We have heard Him; oh, what a difference His words have made in our lives and our preaching. We have beheld Him and touched Him. Don't tell us that He was not real or that He has not risen from the dead."

This Jesus is the source of life. He has revealed to us what real life is.

The concept of the Son as Logos, Word, is also a striking one. While it is true that *logos* is a term used in Greek philosophy for reason, even an eternal reason, I am not sure that John had that in mind when he chose that Greek word to describe the Son. Words are used to communicate. Jesus, the Word made flesh, is not only the one who brought a message of love from God. *He is that message!* He became like me. He was hurt like I am hurt. He taught by words. He taught by miracles. He taught by being Himself.

This Jesus is the *source* of life. He has revealed to us what real life is. Without the message from Jesus and the message of Jesus, we might think life is made up of things. That just is not so. It is that Jesus whom John and the other disciples proclaimed—no phantom—no god using some man's body. *If Christians of any era are to have fellowship with God and with His Son, it can come only through the work of God in Jesus.*

In verse three John tells his audience that this letter is designed to make his joy complete. A father rejoices when good things come to his children. Good things are bound to come to the Christians of Asia Minor if they will appreciate what God has done and is doing in Jesus. Good things will come if these men and women appreciate the salvation that is theirs.

Walking in the Light

1 John 1:5-7

5And this is the message that we have heard from Him and are proclaiming to you that God is light and in Him there is no darkness. 6If we claim that we have fellowship with Him and are walking in the darkness, we are lying and we do not practice the truth. 7But, if we are walking in the light as He is in the light, we have fellowship with one another and the blood of Jesus His son continues to cleanse us from every sin.

The contrast between "light" and "darkness" runs throughout John's Gospel (John 1:4-9; 3:19-21; 5:35; 8:12; 9:5; 11:9-10; 12:35-36, 46) and his letters (1 John 1:5-8; 2:8-10). God enlightens and enlivens. There is nothing in Him that is sordid. If I am His, there will be nothing sordid in my life.

One of the by-words of John's opponents was apparently "we have fellowship with God." That was their way of saying, "We are enlightened. We know. We are saved." Although the opponents of John made these claims for themselves, the claims were never translated into action. Their lifestyle was characterized by darkness. Isn't it interesting how prominent religious leaders and vocal church members often have the same difficulty? "Ah, yes. I am enlightened. I have the Spirit in a special way. My failings? Oh, they don't make any difference. Dishonest business dealings? Sexual immorality? Skimming contributions for personal use?"

The word "fellowship"[4] is used to indicate what two persons or groups hold in common. The Christian's fellowship with God indicates that he or she and God share something special. If we claim to have fellowship with God, our lifestyle will either verify or deny that claim. Since there is nothing in God that is sordid, if we are God's, there will be nothing sordid in our Christian life.

John calls Christians to recognize that fellowship with brothers and sisters in Christ is linked to fellowship with God. That is what makes Christians a body, a family. This relationship with the Father grows out of the saving blood of Jesus. *That relationship is what really matters.* Fellowship is not just a covered-dish dinner after Sunday morning worship. That time of eating and talking is sharing; it is fellowship. But, fellowship is much more. It is tied inextricably to the atoning work of Jesus and its consequences in the lives of believers.

Lifestyle is *direction in life.* John is not as concerned about what I did last as he is about where I am headed. Notice the following phrases in the verses above: walking in the darkness, practicing truth, and walking in the light. The picture of the Christian life is not spiritual Russian roulette. As long as I am headed the right direction, the blood of Jesus *continues* to cleanse me from my sin. I am not gambling on ending up on the right side of that saved/lost line. *God knows my mind. He loves me. He wants me to be saved. He understands my failings. He is on my side.* He is not the God of the Puritan preachers who portrayed the Christian as a spider on the end of a spider web. God held that web over the fires of hell, bouncing it, attempting to make that poor spider fall. I am not that spider! That is not my God.

What a relief! God is not out to "get" me. He knows my heart. Jesus' blood continues to cleanse me of my sin. That is what grace is all about. At the outset of our study of 1 John, we began looking for "marks of a saved person." *John has given his audience the first clue for determining the nature of their relationship with God. I can know that I am saved, forgiven, by examining my direction in life.* Where am I headed? Toward closer communion with God and a life of appreciation for the work of Jesus? Or am I walking in darkness? I can be lost by turning my back on the Lord. Nothing and nobody can separate me from the love of God—that is, nobody but me. I can head the wrong way and walk away from the saving blood of Jesus.

Owning Up

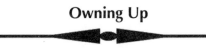

1 John 1:8-10

[8]If we claim that we do not have sin, we are deceiving ourselves and the truth is not in us. [9]If we confess our sins, He [God] is dependable and righteous so that He forgives us the sins and cleanses us from all unrighteousness. [10]If we claim that we have not sinned, we make Him [God] a liar, and His word is not in us.

The Blame Game

Flip Wilson used to portray a character on television who always would say, "The devil made me do it." That idea is not new. When confronted with his transgression, Adam responded to God, "The woman whom you gave me, she . . . ." Adam quickly blamed his wife and ultimately God for his sin. When God turned to Eve, she too passed the buck to Satan. Yet God held all three—Adam, Eve, and Satan—responsible for the fall. John's opponents had convinced themselves that sin was not something you did or committed. They had somehow moved beyond such a mundane thing as sin. They now knew something that positioned them above sin. At its worst, what most would call sin was no more than a bodily act for these enlightened souls; their minds, what was of real importance anyway, had not engaged in that act. They were above sin.

Sin Defined

Sin is real. Due to human predicament we have sin in our lives (1:8); we have sinned in the past with an abiding present consequence. The word "sin"[5] means literally "to miss the mark." That point was brought home to me very clearly several years ago when translating a passage in Plato's *Apology,* his account of Socrates' final defense. Socrates

28

described a man who took aim with his bow and arrow at a target. The man "sinned," that is, he missed the target. All men fall short; they miss the target.

John is concerned that his audience might take sin too lightly. When we sin, we must not move on as if sin were no big deal. Life would become no more than a long stream of sins with no maturing or growth. John tells his audience that anyone who claims to have no sin in his life is deceiving himself and the truth is not in him. His opponents might claim that they were beyond sin; that they knew the grand mysteries, the truth; and that they had fellowship with God. In reality, that simply was not the case. They needed to confess their sins.

> *The Word of God recounts the story of sin, its consequences, and God's plan to deal with it.*

"Wait just a minute, preacher! Did you not say earlier that the Christian life was not a vicious game of Russian roulette? Did you not claim that it was not a chain made up of 'I am lost as an alien sinner, I am baptized, I am now saved, I sin, I am lost, I confess that sin and pray for forgiveness, I am again saved, I sin, I confess that sin and pray, I am saved,' etc.? Is that not what John is saying here? John does say that if we confess our sins God will forgive us. Does this not suggest I am moving back and forth across that imaginary saved/lost line?"

Remember John's opponents. They were people who would contend that they did not sin. They now knew the mystery of the universe, and sin was simply ignorance of this truth. Sin, they would say, was not a part of their lives. The Christian who was struggling to overcome shortcomings in his life would not have this understanding of sin. Guilt could plague his life.

Sin Confessed

The word translated "confess"[6] means literally "to say the same thing." It can also be translated "to acknowledge." In our context "to acknowledge" definitely makes better sense. If these Christians will acknowledge sin in their lives, they can find forgiveness. The blood of Jesus will continue to cleanse them from their sins (1:7b).

If we will not admit that we have sinned and are indeed deserving of the consequences of those sins, how can God shower His grace upon us? To claim that we have no sin is to say that God is a liar. Why? Because God has been acting from the beginning to deal with a problem, which then is not a real problem. The Word of God recounts the story of sin, its consequences, and God's plan to deal with it.

Today people do not claim they are above sin in the same way that the Gnostics did. There is, however, still a problem with taking ownership of sins.

"My boss forced me into a position where I had to . . . ."
"I could not . . . because of my wife."
"If I'm to survive and provide for my family in today's society . . . ."
"But all of my friends at school are . . . ."
"You know the old devil really has really got a hold on me and . . . ."
"Sin really is passé; as long as you don't hurt someone else . . . ."

The Christians to whom John was writing, as well as his opponents, had sin in their lives (1:8). It was a present reality. They also had sinned in the past and would bear the consequences of those sins if they did not acknowledge that they were sinners (1:10). Or as Paul would say, "All have sinned and fallen short of the glory of God" (Romans 3:23). Is that not the universal human predicament? All men have sinned and carry the consequences of past sin. The guilt hangs on. Some people, however, have found the cure for the malady in the blood of Jesus. Those can count on God. He is faithful, utterly dependable. He is just; He will do the right thing.

John in no way wants Christians to minimize the significance of sin. He tells them that he was writing that they might not sin—that is, that sin would not be their way of life. He wants them to direct their lives in the light, striving always to be God's people. This may be John's way of saying with Paul, "Shall we continue to sin that grace may abound? God forbid!" (Romans 6:1).

David was a sinner, and yet, David was a man after God's own heart.

Here again John's concern is lifestyle. That lifestyle is clearly confessional. *We must own up to sin in our lives if we are to be pleasing to God and to have access to the grace that issues from the blood of Jesus.* The structure of verses 7-10 is very much like the Hebrew parallelism of the Psalms, an "A B A B" pattern:

A—"if we walk (present tense in Greek) in the light"

B—"if we claim (aorist tense in Greek) that we have no sin"

A—"if we confess (present tense in Greek) our sins"

B—"if we claim (aorist tense in Greek) that we have not sinned"

The tense of the verb "confess" indicates "keep on confessing." The structure indicates that the life lived in the light will be a life that owns up to brokenness.

The issue is neither saying out loud, "I have sinned," nor coming down the aisle during an invitation song, nor telling someone about your sinful deeds or thoughts. John is concerned about the contrite heart. David was a sinner, and yet, David was a man after God's own heart. Study Psalm 51 and see what that means.

31

Figure 2

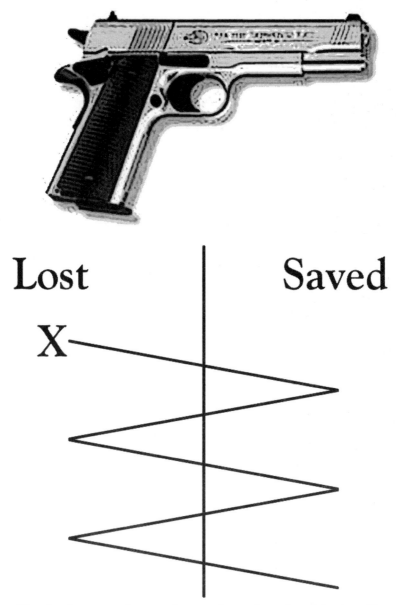

Lost | Saved

X

"Lord, please just let me die on the right side of the line!"

PERSONAL INVENTORY

What direction is my life headed? Am I walking in the light? Do I acknowledge the sin in my life and own up to my failures? Do I depend upon the saving blood of Christ?

LET'S GET PERSONAL

1. Why do you think John would use the metaphors of "light" and "darkness" in both his Gospel and his letters?

2. What does an understanding of 1 John that sees "lifestyle" as John's primary concern do for the Christian who is really struggling to overcome sin in his or her life?

3. How would you respond to the claim of some that this emphasis on "lifestyle" trivializes sin?

4. Discuss the way lifestyle relates to fellowship with God and the way the fellowship with God relates to fellowship with fellow believers?

5. What do you see as the biggest obstacles to fellowship both with God and among believers?

6. Examine Psalm 51 to see what it was about David that made him "a man after God's own heart." Compare your discovery with 1 John 1:9.

7. Read James 5:16. What is different about the call for confession there and the one in 1 John 1:9?

8. Describe what you would conceive to be a confessional lifestyle?

9. Discuss the place of public confession of sin in your life.

Chapter 3

Obey? Yuck!

1 John 2:1-6

> . . . once made perfect, he became the source
> of eternal salvation for all who obey him.
> Hebrews 5:9

A national burger chain aired a commercial that proclaimed, "We do it your way!" The mentality behind the appeal of that commercial pervades our society. We are an autocratic and independent people. We want to do things our own way, make our own decisions, and be our own boss.

The idea of a command being issued is not only unappealing; it is repugnant. When Maynard G. Crebs, sidekick of Dobey Gillis in the '60s TV sitcom, would hear that dirty word "work," he would cringe, cower, and cry out "Work!" Some Christians are tempted to respond in kind when they hear the word "obey."

As Americans we focus on the rights of the individual; we are not interested in hearing about responsibilities or duties. In religion, some proclaim a real conflict between salvation by grace and any call to obedience. There are those in search of a religious commitment where there is no commitment, a faith that has no "I have to."

John helps his audience to see that obedience does have a place in the life of a Christian and that such obedience is a positive command.

Our Advocate

1 John 2:1-2

2:1My little children, I am writing these things to you in order that you might not sin. When anyone does sin, we have an advocate with the Father, Jesus Christ the righteous. 2He is the propitiation for our sins (and not ours only but those of the world as well).

John begins chapter 2 with "my little children," a favorite term of endearment. You can visualize the old man John carried on a litter stopping to place his hand on the head of a member of his congregation and saying, "My little child, love your brothers and sisters."

Most translations render 2:1b, "If anybody does sin . . . ." That is a very literal translation of the Greek text. If you remember what John has just said, you are forced to understand the text as follows: "If any one sins, and he will, we have an advocate with the Father, Jesus Christ, the Righteous One."

The term "advocate" is a special word for John. He used that Greek word to translate what Jesus said of the coming Holy Spirit in John 14 and 16. There Jesus tells His disciples that He must leave so that the Father will send another Advocate[7] (note that Jesus says "another"). When the Advocate (that is, the Spirit) comes, He would remind them of all truth and bring to remembrance all Jesus had taught.

When we do sin, if we will acknowledge those sins, we have someone who will come to our aid, Jesus the Messiah (Christ, which is a Greek word, is the same as Messiah, its Hebrew counterpart). God had planned this event, Messiahship, before the foundation of the world. The promise of that event runs all through the Old Testament. It is the single thread that holds the Bible together. Jesus comes to our aid. It is He who is the *propitiatory* sacrifice for our sins.

Propitiation is a bad word according to many theologians today. They argue that it has lost its original meaning and substitute a more neutral term, "expiation" (RSV), or the phrase, "atoning sacrifice" (NIV). The Greek word behind propitiation originally was used to refer to a sacrifice that would somehow avert the wrath of gods. Admittedly, it sometimes amounted to bribery; however, that idea is foreign to all of the Scriptures. The word is used in the Greek translation of the Old Testament (Septuagint, or LXX) in the Jacob and Esau story to describe the gift that Jacob sent to Esau on his return trip to Canaan. Jacob feared the wrath of his brother. To avert that wrath he sent a gift. While expiation is the *handling of sin*—the satisfaction of the penalty occurred because of sin, propitiation is the *handling of wrath*. The wrath of God is a legitimate idea that runs through  the whole Bible. His wrath is not a temper fit that so often characterizes human beings. It is not the anger that comes because someone broke His favorite plaything. It is righteous indignation. Unlike sacrifices men made to the gods, man could not accomplish the propitiation of God. God Himself had to act to avert His own wrath. He became the propitiatory sacrifice (2:2); He Himself was the propitiatory altar or mercy seat (Romans 3:25). It is by the grace of God and our response to that gift that God's wrath is averted. God was rightly wrathful; He acted to avert that wrath with a sacrifice; *He was that sacrifice!*

Jesus Christ is the Righteous One. There is no other. He has met head-on our problem with sin, not ours alone, but the problem which plagues the whole world. Sin has been dealt a fatal blow in Jesus. My security rests there.

My sin-problem has been dealt with in Jesus' atoning blood. That in no way minimizes my struggle for a God-like, God-pleasing life. Sin cannot be my lifestyle. But, Jesus is my advocate. He is on my side. Hallelujah!

Obedience Proves Knowledge

1 John 2:3-6

³And this is how we know that we have known Him—when

we continue to keep His commandments. 4The one who says, "I have known Him," and yet does not keep His commandments is a liar. The truth is not in this man. 5But whoever keeps His word, in this one the love of God has truly reached maturity. By this we know that we are in Him: 6the one who remains in Him ought to walk just as He (Jesus) walked.

Again we see the by-words of the "bad guys" who are destroying the security of John's audience.

"We know."

"We know Him."

"We possess the truth."

"We are perfect (mature)."

"We are in Him."

John wants his audience to know who really knows God, who really is mature, who really has fellowship with Christ.

The obedience for which John is calling again indicates a lifestyle. John uses a construction[8] to indicate that the one who knows God continues to keep His commandments. John is not calling for sinless perfection, that is, perfect obedience. He has already told his audience that anyone who claims such is making God a liar. John is calling Christians, then and now, to ask some questions about their lives.

"Is my aim to please God, to fulfill His will?

Can I characterize my life as one of obedience or one of self-seeking?

Certainly, I will fall. I will break commandments. But where am I headed?

Is the direction of my life God-ward?"

The Gnostics who claimed special knowledge and relationship with God but lived lives of rebellion were liars. Lifestyle cannot be divorced from relationship. The "religious man" today who claims to possess all sorts of blessings from God but lives a life characterized by sin is a liar.

In verse 5 of chapter 2, John speaks of the love of God.[9] In the present context, John is concerned with the Christian's love for God. He is answering the question: how can we detect the love of God in a Christian's life? John suggests that the solution is simple: Mature love produces an obedient lifestyle.

Children may obey their parents because they fear the consequences of not obeying. The sign of maturity is an obedient lifestyle that grows out of who the child is and the relationship developed with his or her parents. The same is true with regard to obedience toward God.

An important word for John is "perfect." The KJV has translated verse 5, "But whoso keepeth his word, in him verily is the love of God perfected: hereby know we that we are in him." Perfect, for us, normally means without flaw or fault. The Greek word behind it, however, carries the idea of wholeness or completeness, of reaching an intended goal. The Christian's love for God that has reached maturity can be easily identified; it produces an obedient life.

The Christian's love for God that has reached maturity can be easily identified; it produces an obedient life.

If John has in mind, not the Christian's love for God, but God's love for His people, he has indicated that God's love reaches its intended goal when the believer is obedient to God's will. Either way, John is simply echoing what he heard Jesus say:

If you love Me, you will obey what I command

(John 14:15).

He who does not love Me will not obey My teaching

(John 14:24).

Now remain in My love. If you obey My commands,

you will remain in My love (John 15:9-10).

"If you *really* love Me, you will obey." For the disciples to claim that they loved Jesus and yet live lives that were defiant with regard to His teaching was contradictory.

We are led to obey out of love—God's love for us and our love for God. Children often initially respond to their parents out of fear. The goal of a parent is to move the child beyond healthy habits. Initially the slap on the leg or the scolding may be the only stimuli that will produce the correct behavior in the worship assembly. Hopefully, the child will move to correct behavior out of habit simply knowing what the expected behavior is. Ultimately the behavior is internalized. Fear moves to habit which shapes character.

Fear is not an effective long-term motivator. Unfortunately many Christians have stagnated at that point. Most of us initially responded to the gospel out of fear; we did not want to go to hell. Preachers have sometimes reinforced that stagnation by attempting to motivate the Christian to act, be, and evangelize with a steady diet of fear. But all too soon the "hellfire and brimstone" sermon wears off. Other Christians have difficulty moving beyond habit as motivator. They may worship every Sunday, and they may not do so out of fear, but the practice is no more than a comfortable habit. It provides no joy and no growth in fellowship with Father and brother. But in contrast you may see the sister who has learned to appreciate what God has done for her and the brother who knows who he is because of who Jesus is. They obey just like the person motivated by fear or by habit, but that obedience is drastically different.

That obedient lifestyle can best be seen in the life of Jesus Himself. "Whoever claims to live in Him must walk as Jesus did." Generally when we think of the life of Jesus, we think of His sinlessness, of His miracles, of His parables, and of His power. All of that is true. We may move to contemplate the suffering and death of the Savior. Seldom, however, do we think of Him as the paradigm for obedience because, after all, He is God. Yet that is John's emphasis here. Similarly, Paul points the Philippian Christians to Jesus' humility, submission, and obedience:

> Your attitude should be the same as that of Christ Jesus: who, being in very nature God, did not consider equality with God a thing to be grasped, but poured Himself out, taking the form of a slave, being made in the likeness of man. Being found in the form of man, He humbled Himself and became obedient to death—even death on a cross (Philippians 2:6-8).

A humble, obedient lifestyle was Paul's solution for impending divisions in the church at Philippi. It is hard to be a divided church and at the same time be imitating an obedient, humble, serving, pouring-out Savior.

Those bad guys could claim to be in God's favor, but, if their lifestyle did not demonstrate love for God, they were not His. The Christians who were struggling with insecurity could look for this mark of salvation in their own lifestyle.

PERSONAL INVENTORY

What direction is my life headed? Am I walking in the light?

Do I acknowledge the sin in my life and own up to my failures? Do I depend upon the saving blood of Christ?

Can I honestly characterize my life as obedient? Am I really striving to do God's will?

LET'S GET PERSONAL

1. Why is obedience such a distasteful concept?

2. What, if any, difference is there between obedience and legalism?

3. Look at the parables of the Hidden Treasure and the Pearl of Great Price in Matthew 13:44-46. What do they say about the Christian life?

4. What does the understanding of "perfect" suggested in this chapter suggest regarding the meaning of Matthew 5:48? Keep it in the context of Matthew 5:43-48.

5. How do we tend to measure love for God today? Compare this with John's measure of "perfect(ed)" love (1 John 2:5).

6. For John and Paul to use Jesus as an example of obedience is a paradox for many. Why would this be the case?

Chapter 4

Love Him? I Don't Even Like Him!

1 John 2:7-11

. . . "Love your neighbor as yourself."
Matthew 22:39

When Jesus said, "Love one another," the disciples might well have replied, "Lord, that's a mighty tall order. My brother isn't always lovable." By His teaching, especially His parables, Jesus answered, "Neither are you."

Our society has a twisted perspective on what love really is. The problem is compounded because, when we talk about loving our brother, we do not always have a clear understanding of love as it is used in the New Testament. We have a habit of using the term in an empty fashion. We can use love to talk about ice cream, our mates, a child, or, for that matter, anything that gives us pleasure.

Michael Pisarski, age 18, was convinced that he knew what love really was. Michael was a high school dropout. He had been dating Christine Mitchell, age 17, for two and one half years while she was finishing high school. The two broke up; a couple of weeks passed. Finally Michael confronted her in the hall at the high school. Christine's mother had warned the principal that Michael might try to contact her daughter against her wishes. When the principal spotted Michael, he asked him to leave. Michael said, "All I want to do is talk to her for a minute. Then I'll go." Christine began to walk away when Michael reached into his pocket, pulled out a .22

caliber pistol, and fired once. The bullet lodged in Christine's brain. When questioned by the police about the shooting, Michael said, "I was in love with her, and I felt something had to be done. I love her. I love her."[10]

Is that really love? Something is wrong somewhere.

Love and Light

1 John 2:7-11

[7]Loved ones, I am not writing a new commandment to you, but an old commandment, one that you have had from the beginning. The old commandment is the message that you have heard. [8]Yet I am writing a new commandment to you, one which is true in Him and in you. This is so because the darkness is passing away and the true light is already shining.

[9]The one who claims that he is in the light and yet hates his brother is in the darkness to this moment. [10]The one who loves his brother remains in the light, and in him there is no cause for falling. [11]The one who hates his brother is in the darkness and walks in the darkness. He does not know where he is going because the darkness has blinded his eyes.

The word *agape*, translated here as "love,"[11] is a word that was rarely used in the Hellenistic world outside the Greek translation of the Old Testament (Septuagint) and outside our New Testament. When it was used, it often meant no more than "to be satisfied with," "to seek after," or "to desire someone or something." It began to take on a meaning of "to prefer" or "to set one goal or aim above another." The early Christian writers began to use the term to fill a special need. This term came to be used when speakers and authors were describing God's love for us—a kind of love that does not expect anything in return, a love that places someone or something ahead of self. That definition will come out clearly in chapter 3 when John further defines the word love for his readers.

Agape indicates putting a thing or person above other things or persons.[12] It is not primarily an emotion. *Agape* involves action. You cannot command emotions. You can tell me, "Like canned spinach," all day, but I am still not going to like it. I might eat it, but I will not like it. I do not care for the stuff. That is not the way the word *agape* is used. *Agape* is something you can *command*. Paul says, "Love your wives, husband" (Ephesians 5:25). That is a command. A husband might go to a counselor and say, "I don't love my wife anymore." Some counselors say, "Go home and love her." They have issued an instruction, a command: "Treat your wife with respect and honor, putting her needs ahead of your desires."

You cannot command another person to *like* his or her enemies. Yet Jesus commands us to *love*[13] our enemies. In fact, if I am being perfectly honest, I must admit that there are some folks, even among my brothers and sisters, with whom I have some major differences. We may have personality conflicts. We may be at odds. That is not to be preferred, but it is all right as long as I love them. Loving my brothers and sisters means putting their welfare ahead of my own—no easy task. John tells his audience, and in turn us, that loving fellow Christians is one of the marks of a saved person. Do I love my brother or sister? This is not the last time that John provides this admonition for his "little children."

In verse 7 John clarifies this love with:

> Loved ones, I am not writing a new commandment to you, but an old commandment, one that you have had from the beginning. The old commandment is the message that you have heard. Yet I am writing a new commandment to you that is true in Him and in you. This is so because the darkness has passed away and the true light is already shining.

"New commandment . . . old commandment . . ." does that sound familiar? Listen to these words of Jesus from John's Gospel chapter 13 beginning with verse 33. Jesus has just washed the disciples' feet. He then says:

> Little children, I am with you a little while longer, and you will seek Me. As I said to the Jews I now say to you, for where I am going you cannot come. A new commandment I give to you, that you love one another even as I have loved you that

you also love one another. By this all men will know that you are My disciples if you have love one for another.

Does that not sound like our passage? Of course it should; the same man recorded both passages. John was there. He heard Jesus make that statement. Jesus' admonition is very much alive for John. But why does he say that this commandment is both a new commandment and an old commandment? It is easy to understand why it is old. The commandment to love one another, to love your neighbor as yourself, goes all the way back to the book of Leviticus. Why then is it new? Jesus gives it a new meaning. He defines how that love will behave itself by demonstrating it in His own life. It is the "as I have loved you" that makes the commandment new.

Do I live to help my brothers and sisters? Do I really love?

A most important mark of the saved person for John is to be found in the question "Do I love my brother?" John is only beginning his discussion of love for brother here. Loving one's brother is a theme that recurs throughout this letter. Later on in chapter 3 and again in chapter 4, John will return to the topic.

John tells us that the one who loves his brother abides in the light and there is no cause for stumbling in him.[14] Note that John says that he abides in the light—one of the ways for John to say that he is saved. "There is no cause" for whom "to stumble"? If you put your brother's welfare ahead of your own, there is no danger that you are going to trip him up, and one major obstacle has been removed from your own path. You will be looking out for your brother. The false teachers who claimed to have special knowledge and to be above the ordinary folks did not really care about their brothers and sisters. In fact they were putting them down. "Oh, you're just ordinary. I'm important because I know the mystery. You see I'm one of these Gnostics. I know, and I'm better, and I'm more important." Notice that my attitude toward my brother also speaks of my direction in life.

Those who hate their brothers or sisters are in the darkness. Again that is direction. The word for "hate" in the original language indicates a continued action. That is the person's disposition. Such a person is walking in the darkness and is headed the wrong way. Those who hate do not know where they are going because the darkness has blinded their eyes. Everyone knows someone who hates another person so desperately that he or she cannot recognize the truth.

The lesson Jesus taught His disciples that last fateful night, recorded by John in chapters 13-15 of his Gospel, had sunk very deeply into the life of John. Now he is trying to share that lesson with his audience. Here again is the old man, as the tradition goes, who is carried around on a litter and reaches out to pat the folks on the head and to say, "Love one another, my little children."

Love is not easy to practice. It stretches us as Christians. Going the second mile and turning the other cheek will never be easy. But, then, being like the One who loved me and sent His Son to die for me is bound to stretch me.

PERSONAL INVENTORY

What direction is my life headed? Am I walking in the light?

Do I acknowledge the sin in my life and own up to my failures? Do I depend upon the saving blood of Christ?

Can I honestly characterize my life as obedient? Am I really striving to do God's will?

Do I live to help my brothers and sisters? Do I really love?

LET'S GET PERSONAL

1. Is it possible to like all Christians?

2. What difficulties arise when you try to love someone you don't like, for example, an enemy?

3. Look at the use of word *agape/agapao* in 2 Peter 2:15 and in 1 John 2:15. How do these passages increase your understanding of the meaning of the word? Is *agape* always used in a positive way?

4. Is it possible for a person to be so blinded by his lifestyle, walking in the darkness, that he cannot see the way out?

5. Discuss Matthew 5:38-48 in terms of a call from Jesus for the disciples to exercise *agape.*

Chapter 5

You Are a Winner!
You Know What Matters

1 John 2:12-17

. . . I consider everything a loss compared to the surpassing greatness of knowing Christ Jesus my Lord, for whose sake I have lost all things.

Philippians 3:8a

A Christian stood before an angry Roman emperor, who yelled,

"I will banish you!"

"You cannot," responded the Christian, "because the whole world is my Father's."

"Then I will slay you," said the emperor.

"That doesn't frighten me because my life is hid with Christ in God. I have no fear of those who can destroy the body but have no power to destroy the soul."

"Then," retorted the emperor, "I will take away all your treasures."

The Christian responded, "You cannot do that for my treasure is in heaven where moth and rust do not corrupt."

The frustrated emperor finally said, "I will drive you away from all men. You will have no friend left to be near you."

The Christian quietly affirmed his faith: "You can't do that either. I have a friend from whom you cannot separate me. Nothing can do that. Neither life nor death nor things present nor things to come can separate me from His love. I cannot lose."

Oh, to learn what really matters! Oh, to know that I have already won the war in Christ Jesus!

That gentle, fatherly old man, John, may have worried that his little children would be discouraged by the harsh words he had just used (1:6, 8, 10; 2:4, 9-11)—words that were really intended for his opponents. But how would John's flock hear them?

John responds with what appears to be poetry.

Knowing Him

1 John 2:12-14

¹²I am writing to you, little children,
>because your sins are forgiven for His name's sake.
¹³I am writing to you, (fathers) mature Christians,
>because you know Him who has been from the beginning.
I am writing to you, young people,
>because you have overcome the evil one.
I have written to you, children,
>because you know the Father.
¹⁴I have written to you, (fathers) mature Christians,
>because you know Him who has been from the beginning.
I have written to you, young people,
>because you are strong and the Word of God abides in you
>and you have overcome the evil one.

Do you see two major sections? Each of the two stanzas addresses, in the same order, children, mature Christians (fathers), and young people.

The First Stanza

The term "children" is likely used to encompass all Christians whom John is addressing—young and old, male and female, married or single, slave or free. These Christian brothers and sisters are John's children (1 John 2:18, 28; 3:7, 18; 4:4; 5:21).

In each stanza after addressing the church as a whole, John narrows his audience to address older folks and younger folks.

It is not apparent why John uses the present tense, "I am writing," in the first stanza only to change to the past tense, "I have written," in the second stanza. It may simply be a stylistic change. The repetition of subjects and verbs make it clear that we are dealing with poetic discourse.

By the way, it is not necessary to think that John intends to ignore the ladies in the church when he address only "fathers" and "young men." In Greek, if you desire to address a mixed group (both men and women), you will often use masculine nouns and pronouns. This may be all that John is doing here. He may be using the term "fathers" to refer to those who had been Christians for some time and should exhibit maturity. The word translated "young men" in most English translations would then refer to those who are young in the faith.

John begins, "I am writing to you, children, because your sins are forgiven you for His name sake." Your sins, not will be, not might be, but *are* forgiven. "I don't care what those false teachers say. Your sins are forgiven now." Again John emphasizes Christian security. Living the Christian life is not a game of Russian roulette!

"I'm writing to you, (fathers) mature Christians, because you know Him who has been from the beginning." The key word for the false teachers, the Gnostics, is "know." They would say, "We know. We know the mystery." John tells these Christians, "The false teachers don't really know. You know what really matters. Don't let anybody fool you. You know the one who's been from the beginning."

"The one who has been from the beginning" undoubtedly points to Jesus. First John begins, "what was from the beginning, what we have heard . . . seen . . . beheld . . . handled . . . ." (1:1). There John is proclaiming the Word of Life, Jesus. Similarly, John begins his Gospel with: "In the beginning was the Word, and the Word was with God, and the Word was God."

"You," John is saying, "know, Jesus. Don't let anybody tell you otherwise. He is the one who matters. His blood continues to cleanse you from all sin."

"I'm writing to you, young people, because you have overcome the evil one." If I were talking with a junior or senior high school class, many of them would have the perfect illustration of John's point on their feet. A popular brand of athletic shoes is *Nike*, the shoe of champions. *Nike* comes form the same Greek root family that is translated both "overcomes" and "victory" in our text (see also 1 John 5:4, 5).[15] Christians are champions. How can these Christians, indeed all Christians, know that they will win? It is their trust, our trust, in the saving work of God in Jesus that has produced this victory.

The war was not over for these Christians, but they had won the decisive battle fought by Jesus. They were, thus, winners. They had overcome. "Young people, I'm writing to you because the victory is yours. You've overcome the evil one."

The Second Stanza

John begins the second cycle or stanza with "I have written to you, children . . . ."[16] In the first stanza John told the (fathers) mature Christians that they knew the one from the beginning, Jesus. Now he tells the whole church that they know the Father. "I have written to you, children, because you know the Father." "To know" does not mean "to be familiar with." In Hebrew and in Greek, the word "to know" signifies an intimate relationship. Here "know" is used of the relationship between the believer and God. These Christian men and women have intimate relationship with the Father.

"I have written to you, (fathers) mature Christians, because you know Him who has been from the beginning." John has already said that in the first stanza. Why the repetition? Knowing is important to John's audience. These older Christians knew the one who makes victory sure. What their opponents knew or claimed to know was insignificant.

"I have written to you, young people, because you are strong and the Word of God abides in you and you've overcome the evil one." John repeats his admonition that these younger Christians are going to win the battle. This time, though, he tells them that they are strong.

"John, we are strong? What do you mean John? We feel our

weaknesses, our failures. We feel like losers." To that John would reply, "The gospel, God's Word, His message of good news, abides in you. He, through it, is changing your life. Don't let anyone get you down."

Now, that is a message Christians need to hear today. It is so easy for me to get down on myself. When I slip and fall, when folks make themselves out to be more than they really are, and when I feel small, I need to know that I have won the battle.

How then can I, a Christian, relate to the world around me? Can I love God and yet grab all the pleasure this world has to offer? Can I be a Christian and a yuppie at the same time? How does the Christian live *in* this world yet not be *of* it? John tells us that it is all a matter of priorities. What really matters to you?

Do Not Love the World

1 John 2:15-17

15Do not love the world, nor the things in the world. If anyone loves the world, the love of the Father is not in him. 16For all that is in the world—the lust of the flesh and the lust of the eyes and the pride of life—is not from the Father, but is from the world. 17And the world is passing away along with its lust, but the one who does the will of God abides forever.

The World

"Do not love the world nor the things that are in the world." Does that mean that I have to stop singing "This Is My Father's World"? Can I no longer admire nature? Just what am I to make of this passage?

What does John mean by "world" and "the things that are in the world"? John does not mean trees and grass and moun-tains and stars at night. The heavens declare God's glory, and the earth is His handiwork (Psalm 19:1). John does not mean those who inhabit this earth. God sent His Son to die for all of those people (John 3:16, 17). There is nothing wrong with loving people or with appreciating creation. In fact God calls us to do both.

Note that worldliness does not reside in things but in our obsession with them.

John is calling these Christians not to love a system ruled by Satan, a *system* that places things and self above God. The *New English Bible* says it well, "Do not set your heart on the godless world" (1 John 2:15). John clarifies this meaning in verse 16. Sin rules the way of the world. It is what man has done and continues to do to creation because of his fallen nature. Jesus warned His disciples that no man can serve two masters. He calls the opposing master "mammon" (Matthew 6:24). John calls this opposing master "the world."

The World's Traps

John clarifies what he means by "world." He tells them, "Here are the things that are in the world: the lust of the flesh, the lust of the eyes, and the boastful pride of life." The word "lust" in the original language[17] is sometimes translated "desire" (2 Corinthians 5:2; 7:7, 11; Philippians 1:23; 4:17; 1 Thessalonians 2:17; 3:6; 1 Timothy 3:1; 2 Timothy 1:4). Does that surprise you? The basic meaning of the word is "a craving." If used in a positive sense, the Greek word is translated "desire." If it is "the cravings of sinful man," desiring something you are not supposed to have, then it is translated "lust." The lust of the flesh, the lust of the eyes, the boastful pride of life—these have been called the avenues of temptation. They are the hooks Satan uses to get us on his line. John may not have intended to give an all-inclusive list of those hooks, but it is difficult to conceive of another way for sin to come.

"The lust of the flesh" is the craving for satisfaction of physical appetites in an illegitimate way, putting those appetites ahead of the will of God. "The lust of the eyes" refers to the mental craving for the possession of things, putting the acquisition of those things ahead of the will of God. "The arrogant pride of life"[18] is the quest for the right public image and for personal power, putting that image and power ahead of the will of God. Note that worldliness does not reside in things but in our obsession with them.

Satan used those same hooks to catch Eve (Genesis 3:1-6). She saw that the fruit was pleasant to the eyes, good to eat, and desirous to make you wise—the lust of the eyes, the lust of the flesh, and the pride of life.

Does my relationship with God and spiritual things take precedence over the things the world would have me treasure?

Satan tried the same technique with Jesus in the wilderness (Luke 4:1-13). The first temptation was "Turn these stones into bread"—meet your physical needs in an inappropriate way, the lust of the flesh. Next Satan took Jesus to a high mountain and said, "Look at all the land out there. How would You like to rule over all that land? Take a shortcut and bow down to worship me"—the lust of the eyes. Finally, he takes Jesus to the pinnacle of the temple. "If You're God's Son, throw yourself down from the temple. You know those angels are going to come and catch you. I mean they have to, You're God's son. Show who You are!"—pride of life.

Satan's attack has not changed. The world would have us believe, "We have needs, and those needs must be met. There are things out there that would make us happy, and we need to acquire them. My status is tied to my possessions, my accomplishments, and my power." But, it isn't so! That is our struggle. It is so real.

"The world is passing away and also its desires, but the one who does the will of God abides forever." Where are my priorities, what really matters to me? Doing the will of God provides meaning. Jesus put it this way, "Seek first the reign of God . . . , and God will take care of all of these things" (Matthew 6:33).

PERSONAL INVENTORY

What direction is my life headed? Am I walking in the light?

Do I acknowledge the sin in my life and own up to my failures? Do I depend upon the saving blood of Christ?

Can I honestly characterize my life as obedient? Am I really striving to do God's will?

Do I live to help my brothers and sisters? Do I really love?

Where do things fall in my list of priorities? Does my relationship with God and spiritual things take precedence over the things the world would have me treasure?

LET'S GET PERSONAL

1. How important is it for the Christian to feel like a winner?

2. What things in the world today can cause the Christian to feel like a loser?

3. Do you as a Christian ever reach a stage when you have won the struggle over priorities?

4. What is the difference the way the world measures worth and the way the Christian should measure worth?

5. What should be the Christian's view toward the world and the things that are in it?

Chapter 6
Watch Out for the Antichrist
1 John 2:18–3:3

For no matter how many promises
God has made, they are "Yes" in Christ.
2 Corinthians 1:20a

There is a knock at the door. You open the door to meet a man and a woman nicely dressed with a fistful of pamphlets. After the normal pleasantries, the man quotes a passage from 1 Timothy, "But the Spirit explicitly says that in later times some will fall away from the faith paying attention to deceitful spirits and doctrines of demons . . . (4:1-3)." He then says, "Don't you believe that passage describes the world today? The end is around the corner. The antichrist is near, and we have discovered who he is."

That is not an uncommon happening. Many religious people today have developed strange theologies by treating the Bible like a jigsaw puzzle. They put together passages that have no logical connection other than an assumed mention of the end of time. Typically "the man of lawlessness" of 2 Thessalonians 2 is conjoined with "the antichrist" of 1 John 2. That concoction is mixed with the "beast," "666," and the thousand-year reign of Revelation 20. For good measure to that combination is added a pinch of the later days from 1 Timothy. And voila! Someone proclaims, "We've just discovered the man who unlocks the mystery. We now know when Jesus is going to return."

We cannot treat the Bible in such a fashion. It is not a collection of 999 disjointed affirmations that are to be pieced together to discover rules for Christian living, order for worship, and a program for the end times. By looking at each passage in its context and examining the message it brought to the original audience, we can ascertain the message of a passage and will learn that many passages that are linked like those above do not go together.

Beware of the Antichrists

1 John 2:18-23

[18]Little children, it is the last hour. Just as you have heard that antichrist is coming, so now many antichrists have arisen. Thus, we know that it is the last hour. [19]They went out from us, but they were not really of us. For, if they really had been of us, they would have remained with us; however, in order that it might be made clear that they are not of us, they went out.

[20]But you have an anointing from the Holy One, and you all know. [21]I have not written to you because you do not know the truth, but because you do know it and because no lie comes from the truth. [22]Who is the liar but the one who denies that the Christ is Jesus? This one is the antichrist, the one who denies the Father and the Son. [23]Whoever denies the Son does not have the Father; the one who acknowledges the Son has the Father also.

The Antichrists

Notice that John says, "antichrist is coming" and then goes on to say, "now many antichrists have arisen." That does not sound like someone for whom we should be looking for today. We would naturally expect the culprit to arise in John's own day.

Another clue for understanding the antichrist is to be found in the meaning of the word itself—*anti* "against" plus *Christos* "Christ." The antichrists stand against Jesus as the

Christ (cf., 2:22). In the historical context of 1 John, an antichrist would oppose the Christ saying that Jesus and the Christ were not the same. The Docetics and Gnostics claimed that Christ, an inferior deity, adopted Jesus' body but left before Jesus died on the cross. Thus, we are left with a Jesus who was not fully God and fully human. That is heresy.

John says that these false teachers are coming and are present at the last hour. If there is a Messiah, there will be those who oppose Him. The last hour for Jews could be any time after the arrival of the Messiah. Once the Messiah arrives, the last days have begun. History takes a 90-degree turn. A new era has begun. It makes no difference whether that era lasts one year, 1000 years, 2000 years, or a million years; it is still the last hour.

"They went out from us, but they weren't really from us. For if they had been of us, they would have remained with us. But they went out from us in order that they might be shown that they are not of us." This passage is frequently used to teach "once saved, always saved." It is claimed, "If someone falls away, he was really never saved in the first place. It is impossible to fall." Christian security is real. The possibility of turning your back on Jesus is also real. Again, let's put the passage in its historical context. Suppose there are folks who worship as Christians, who claim to be Christians. They say, "We are with you," but contend that Jesus is not fully God and fully human and that God really was not working in Jesus. That is serious.

The foundation stone of the Christian religion is the fact that God was working in Jesus to save the world. If someone denies that, he was never a Christian. The topic under discussion is not falling away. It is not a declaration that leaving always proves you were never really saved. That was not the issue at hand. These folks do not hold to the one central doctrine of the Christian religion. You are not a Christian in any way if you deny the reality of the atonement. These men claimed to be Christians but denied that one teaching which makes all the difference.

"They went out to make it clear that they weren't really of

us." This group of false teachers was initially a part of the body. They became a distinct splinter group by the end of the first century. The believers' acknowledgment of the atoning work of God was what really made them a body, the church.

The Anointing

"You have an anointing from the Holy One and you all know." "You know what matters," he says. "Don't let them fool you. They may claim to know, but you know. You have an anointing." There is a pun in the Greek text that the English reader is unlikely to see. A very literal translation will help: "Little children, it's the last hour . . . . You've heard that the anti-anointed-one[19] is coming, but you have an anointing."[20] Verse 22 continues "Who is the liar but the one who denies that Jesus is the Anointed One[21]? This is the anti-anointed-one." The pun in Greek is clear: anointing, Anointed One, or Christ; and against-the-anointed-one or antichrist. All three words are from the same Greek root.

"You have an anointing." John will clarify what he means by that word "anointing" later in chapters 2, 3, and 4 (2:27; 3:24–4:3; 4:13). The anointing can be seen as either the Holy Spirit who dwells within the Christian or the message of Jesus the Christ. The context favors the Holy Spirit. Further discussion of the significance of the indwelling Spirit will appear in chapters 8 and 9. John offers words of encouragement to his spiritual children: "The Spirit indwells you; you know; you have what it takes; you have a special relationship with the Son and with the Father."

The Acknowledgment

John is not writing this letter because his audience does not know about Jesus. They know the story of Jesus, and that story has changed their lives. He is writing so that they will not forget the significance of that story and so that the false teachers will not get them down.

John's definition of "antichrist" becomes clear. Anyone who denies that Jesus is the Christ, who denies the relationship between the Father and the Son, who says that the Son and the

Father are not God with a capital "G," that person is an antichrist. That fits the description of the bad guys John is combating— false teachers who said that Jesus' body was adopted by a lower deity and that the Father, the supreme God, and the Creator were different entities.

Anyone who denies the Father and the Son is the antichrist.

Anyone who denies the Father and the Son is the antichrist. There are religious groups today that deny that Jesus is fully God. They contend that He is a lesser deity, a god, but not really God. Such a movement cannot be called Christian. Members of these groups can *call* themselves Christians, but they are no more Christians than the false teachers John was refuting.

John continues, "Whoever denies the Son does not have the Father. The one who confesses the Son has the Father also." The word there translated "confess"[22] can be translated "acknowledge." The same word appeared earlier in 1 John (1:9). Acknowledging Jesus is more than saying something out loud at the time of your baptism. It is a whole lifestyle that acknowledges Jesus as God's Son. Confession of Jesus is a lifestyle. When Jesus said, "Deny Me, and I'll deny you. Confess Me before men; I'll confess you before the Father," He was talking about a whole life. It is about saying something, but it is more than just voicing a belief. It is living a life that acknowledges Him as the Christ, as God's Son.

Remaining Forever

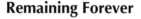

1 John 2:24-25

[24]What you heard from the beginning, let it remain in you. If what you heard from the beginning remains in you, you will remain both in the Son and in the Father. [25]And this is the promise He promised—life eternal.

What does John mean by "What you heard from the beginning"? John undoubtedly has in mind the gospel message that these Christians heard at the very beginning of their Christian pilgrimage, that is, what the apostles taught them. John would have them ask, "Am I abiding in the apostolic teaching?" Not only does this question serve as an evaluation of the Christian's relationship with God, but also later John will use this as a test to mark the false teachers (4:6).

God has made a promise to all believers, and that promise is eternal life. One of the troubling signs for the direction of the church today is what comes from its pulpits. While preaching in Indiana, I watched with fascination the sermon topics of the preacher for a large denomination. For thirteen weeks his sermons were based on *Jonathan Livingston Seagull.* I thought to myself, "Oh, how ridiculous! That will never happen among the churches of Christ." I have been disappointed to learn that something quite similar is happening. Sermons are preached which have very little connection to a Biblical text. The Scripture is used to illustrate the sermon rather than the sermon arising out of Scripture. It would seem that the Scripture really does not matter. The Bible, the apostolic teaching, needs to make a difference. Sometimes the best we can hope is that a preacher will use the text as an illustration on equal par with the jokes he tells, the illustrations he uses, or the pop-psychology he cites. The message does not arise out of a Biblical text, but is imposed upon it.

John says, "Listen, folks. You know the truth. You've been taught it. You have learned it, the message of Jesus. You heard it from the apostles. Hang on to it. That's what makes a difference. Don't worry about all these philosophies these folks make up."

God has made a promise to all believers, and that promise is eternal life. For John, eternal life is not quantity of life or duration of life. It is quality of life, real life. That promise of God is sure. He keeps His word. The false teachers who are trying to lead these believers astray may be causing them to doubt that promise. John will not have that. The promise of God is eternal life. God promised it so the Christian need not worry about it.

Abiding Anointing

1 John 2:26-27

²⁶These things I have written to you concerning those who are trying to lead you astray. ²⁷As for you, the anointing which you received from Him abides in you and you have no need that anyone teach you. But just as His anointing teaches you concerning all things (and it is true, and it is not a lie), and just as it taught you, remain in Him.

The deceivers would have these Christians to believe that they must know their dandy mystery, understand their gods, and comprehend their truth that matter is bad and spirit good. To that John responds, "That stuff is not important. In fact, it is not even true." What really matters is abiding in the teaching that gave you the promise in the first place.

John has countered any elitism of false teachers: "It is not so for the bad guys, but as for you, the anointing you received from Him abides in you." Paul said it this way, "You were sealed in Him with the Holy Spirit of promise, who is given as a down payment of our inheritance until the redemption of God's possession to the praise of His glory" (Ephesians 1:13b-14). All Christians receive the indwelling of the Holy Spirit at their new birth. We will never really understand how the Spirit works; but He is ours, He is within us, and He is at work transforming us.

Special people are anointed. Sick people may be anointed. Special guests are anointed. Kings are anointed. "You," John says, "are anointed."

This anointing abides in believers. There is no need for anyone to teach them about God's work in their lives; they know it. They need to be reminded, but they do not need to be taught. Although the subjective component of the Christian's faith must be grounded in the objective, there is a place for the subjective, the sense of experiencing deep down in our being a relationship with God.

John is not suggesting that the Spirit tells Christians everything they are to do and that they have no need for study. The

Spirit is at work appropriating that message for the Christian's life, transforming his character, developing the fruit of the Spirit (Galatians 5:22-25).

God's anointing, the indwelling Holy Spirit, is teaching believers all things—not everything about everything—but the things that matter. This anointing is dependable. The Spirit will teach *if* we will listen. Learning to listen is not easy. It requires the constant search for the will of God in all that we do.

Paul warned the Christians at Thessalonica not to quench the Spirit (1 Thessalonians 5:19). The Christians to whom John wrote had already learned from the Spirit the importance of remaining in relationship with God.

God's Children

1 John 2:28–3:3

[28]And now, little children, remain in Him, so that when He appears, we might have confidence and might not be ashamed before Him at His coming. [29]If you know that He is righteous, you know that everyone who does righteousness has been born of Him.

[3:1]See how great a love the Father has given to us, that we might be called children of God! And that is what we are! For this reason the world does not know us, because it did not know Him. [2]Beloved, we are now children of God. It has not yet become clear what we shall be. But we know that, when He appears,[23] we shall be like Him, because we shall see Him just as He is. [3]And everyone who has this hope fixed on Him purifies himself, just as He is pure.

John recognized that his audience was composed of "not-yet beings." That is part of the human predicament. Christians have been redeemed, yet they struggle to remain free. They have been set free from sin, yet they sin. Despite that "not-yet-ness," John offers confidence and security to those who "remain in Him." At Jesus' coming, we who maintain relationship with Him will not shrink in fear, but rather will approach Him with confidence. Again, John is calling for a lifestyle. On the judgment day, that lifestyle makes it possible for the Christian to walk up to Jesus and say, "Ah, I've been longing to see you."

If God is righteous (and He is), we who are in relationship with Him will "do" or "practice righteousness." He cannot do otherwise. John does not claim that the Christian does everything right. Nor does he say that the Christian will never do wrong. It is direction in life that indicates relationship.

We are really special people—special, not because of our own merits, but because God has called us His children. He loved us when we were not lovable. He adopted us when we were not cute, little, or innocent. The Gnostics could claim whatever they wished, but Christians have what is really significant, relationship with the Father, a relationship that transforms lifestyle.

We are really special people — special, not because of our own merits, but because God has called us His children.

The world will not appreciate the Christian whose life is tied to a righteous Savior, One whom the world did not accept. During His lifetime, Jesus warned His disciples that they should not expect acceptance. He said, "Listen! They persecuted Me; they'll persecute you. They turned a deaf ear to Me; they'll turn a deaf ear to you" (John 15:20ff.). If we are God's people, we have to expect some rejection and persecution. All of us would like to be liked. But, there will be some folks who will be uncomfortable around you who are God's person.

The Christian's "not-yet-ness" again surfaces when we think about life after death. Do you ever wonder what it will be like on the other side of the judgment day? What kind of body will I have? How will I be able to recognize other people?

John says he does not have all the answers to life after death either. For John, that really is not important. We will be like Jesus. What more can we ask? If we will be like the Lord, what more must we know? We will see Him just as He is.

John tells these believers that "everyone who has this hope

fixed on Him purifies himself just as He is pure." It is unfortunate that the word hope is blurred by the flippant fashion in which the term is used today. I really hope I'll win the Publisher's Clearing House Sweepstakes. I buy a stamp and mail in every entry form; however, I really do not believe I will ever win. I would like to win and at times fantasize about what I would do if I did win. But I am not making any arrangements to spend the money.

The hope of salvation is not a one in a million chance of being saved.

There is a danger that, as people talk about the Christian's hope, the Publisher's Clearing House Sweepstakes becomes the operative model. When someone prays, "Lord, we thank you for giving us the hope of salvation," is he simply thanking God for the "outside chance" of salvation, for a "shot in the dark"? The hope of salvation is not a one in a million chance of being saved. The Christian is already "spending the money."

Hope means steadfast assurance or anxious awaiting. It pertains to something I know will happen. I am just waiting for the object of that hope.

What makes hope so sure? Faith! The author of Hebrews taught that "Faith is the substance of things hoped for, the evidence of things not seen" (Hebrews 11:1). That passage might well be translated: "Now faith gives substance to the things hoped for. It makes real (proves), things never seen."

The Christian's hope is fixed on Jesus. He will be like Jesus. That hope will transform his life. He will strive to be pure because his Lord is pure. He will have something others lack, a sense of priority, a sense of direction.

PERSONAL INVENTORY

What direction is my life headed? Am I walking in the light?

Do I acknowledge the sin in my life and own up to my failures? Do I depend upon the saving blood of Christ?

Can I honestly characterize my life as obedient? Am I really striving to do God's will?

Do I live to help my brothers and sisters? Do I really love?

Where do things fall in my list of priorities? Does my relationship with God and spiritual things take precedence over the things the world would have me treasure?

Do I acknowledge Jesus as the Christ, the Son of God, in all that I say and do?

Do I abide in the apostolic teaching? Does the message of the Bible govern my life and my thoughts?

Do I let God work in my life? Do I search for His will or do I quench His Spirit?

Do I let God work in my life? Do I search for His will or do I quench His Spirit?

LET'S GET PERSONAL

1. What danger do you see for the Christian who is always searching for "the antichrist," an evil man, in order to discover the time of the second coming?

2. What makes the deity and the humanity of Jesus such important doctrines or elements of faith?

3. Name religious groups today that would deny the deity (or the "full deity") of Jesus.

4. What does it mean to confess Jesus?

5. Do you feel the Bible and its message of God's work in Jesus has slipped from being the focal point in churches today? If so, why and how can this malady be corrected? If not, how can we keep our focus where it ought to be?

6. What competing philosophies today would seek to replace the apostolic message of God's saving work?

7. Discuss places in your life that the tension of "not-yet-ness" becomes significant.

8. Discuss the idea of adoption in Galatians 4:1-7 as it relates to 1 John 2:28–3:3.

9. Consider how the definition of "hope" given in this chapter affects your understanding of the following passages: Romans 8:22-25; 1 Peter 3:15; 1 Timothy 1:1; Titus 2:11-14.

10. Persecution today seldom takes the form it did in the firs century. How should the Christian with a transformed lifestyle expect to be treated by the world?

11. Why are questions about exactly what will happen at the moment of death or of the resurrection so crucial to many Christians?

Chapter 7

Practice Makes . . .

1 John 3:4-15

*The Spirit gives life; the flesh counts for nothing. The words I
have spoken to you are spirit and they are life.*
John 6:63

"Practice makes perfect." Well, that depends on what you
practice and how you practice it. In response to that someone
might say, "Perfect practice makes perfect." John makes an
even bolder claim: PRACTICE MAKES A PERSON. In 1 John 3,
John again emphasizes the practice of sin and the practice of
righteousness.

Doing and Being

1 John 3:4-10

⁴Everyone who practices sin also practices lawlessness;
indeed, sin is lawlessness. ⁵And you know that He [Jesus]
appeared in order that He might take away sins, and in Him
there is no sin. ⁶No one who abides in Him keeps on sinning.
No one who keeps on sinning has seen Him or knows Him.

⁷Little children, let no one lead you astray. Everyone who
practices righteousness is righteous just as He [Jesus] is righteous.
⁸The one who practices sin is of the devil, because the devil has
been sinning from the beginning. For this reason the Son of God
appeared, namely that He might destroy the works of the devil.

⁹Everyone who has been begotten of God does not practice sin, because His seed abides in him. He cannot continue in sin because he has been begotten of God. ¹⁰In this way the children of God and the children of the devil are obvious: everyone who does not practice righteousness is not of God, the same is true of the one who does not love his brother.

Sin Is Breaking the Law

It is important for John's hearers to see the connection between "practicing sin" and "practicing lawlessness." According to the false teachers sin was not to be seen as the act of doing something wrong. That would be a matter of indifference, something your body would do, an act that really did not involve your essence—your mind. Once a person came to know the mystery, he was home free. He already had a resurrected body. He really did no sin. Earlier in the letter, to such false teachers John said, "If you say you have not sinned, you make God a liar."

Sin is breaking the law; it is lawlessness. Jesus' goal in coming to the earth was to deal with man's sin problem. To accomplish that Jesus lived a sinless life and then went on to die on a cross. If a man lives as if there is no law—no right and wrong—and practices sin, he treats God's saving act as though it were rubbish.

Beware of False Teachers

False teachers in John's day who claimed to have seen God through some special mystery and to have known Him were liars. Christians ought not be fooled by those in any age who claim to know God and be in close association to Him yet live sinful lives. A sinful lifestyle never characterizes the Christian.

Many translations of verse 6 might lead the modern reader to imagine that John was contradicting Himself—for example, "Whoever abideth in him sinneth not" (KJV); or "No one who abides in him sins" (RSV). In chapter one verse 8, John said, "If we say that we have no sin, we deceive ourselves and the truth is not in us." In the same chapter verse 10, he said, "If we say that we have not sinned, we make God a liar and His Word is not in us." How can he now say, "No one who sins abides in Him" and "No one who sins has seen Him or knows Him"?

There are those who contend that, when you first become a Christian, you may sin. However, somewhere along the line, the Christian receives a second work of grace, an extra "shot" of the Spirit, enabling him to reach sinless perfection. From then on, if he does something wrong, it was not his inner self that sinned. Perhaps environment or peers caused a slip, but the Christian no longer wills to sin. He is above sin.

If you serve a righteous Savior, you will strive to be righteous yourself.

"No one who abides in Him continues to sin." That is what John is saying. The grammar in the original language permits, in fact demands, that interpretation. John is again calling for an examination of lifestyle, direction.

In John's day, false teachers claimed to know God. But, their lives were filled with sin. The natural response should be "Something is wrong. Everyone sins, but that is not the problem here. We are not just talking about a sin; we are talking about a lifestyle."

Television evangelists have come to the forefront in recent years for certain improprieties. If the impropriety were a single act or even several "unconnected" sins, that would be one thing. But you must question the ministry, the sincerity, and the relationship with God of one whose life is filled with sin. The natural response is, "This looks like lifestyle to me."

John's concern here is not with a one-time event or the struggle to "lick" a problem. As a Christian, I want to avoid the one-time sin. I don't want to sin at all. Sin will, however, occur in my life. I cannot minimize it. What really matters though is the direction I am headed. I can really get down on myself by piling up all of the one-time events. I can buffet myself with guilt, never forgiving myself for those shortcomings. I look back and see that sin I committed ten years ago. I should not have done it; I knew better! I can focus on my own failure;

security goes out the window. Or, I can rely on the blood of Jesus, get up, and strive to do His will.

At the other extreme, I can make individual sins so insignificant that they come to characterize my life. I must be certain that I am walking in the light. I must own up to my sins.

"The one who practices righteousness is righteous just as Jesus is righteous." What you *do* is what you *are*. What you practice makes you. If you serve a righteous Savior, you will strive to be righteous yourself. If you practice sin, your allegiance is also clear. You are of the devil. He first missed the mark in the beginning. His goal since the beginning has been to get man to sin and so to worship him. Jesus came to deal with the devil's work once and for all.

Several years ago I found myself in a classical Greek class at the University of Kentucky, translating Plato. I never expected to find a good sermon illustration. Plato records Socrates' speech to defend himself before a court of his peers in Athens. In that speech, Socrates tells of an archer who takes aim and "sins." Socrates would not have us believe that the archer did or thought something bad. He was simply saying that the archer missed the target; he sinned.

Sinning is missing the target, not living up to God's high goal for our lives. The false teacher can try his best to minimize the significance of wrong acts—deeds done or deeds left undone. They are still sins.

God's Seed Within

The one who is born of God has God's seed within him. With God in him, he cannot keep on sinning. He must either turn his back on God and give up relationship with Him, or change his life. "No one born of God practices sin because His seed abides in him. He cannot sin because he is born of God." Again, translations may mislead modern readers, causing them to think that John is demanding a sinless life of the Christian. But again, John is saying that Christians cannot keep on sinning. God is working in them. They cannot live a sinful lifestyle. If they continue in relationship with God, something just will not let them do that.

It becomes obvious whether you are of God or of the devil. Lifestyle tells it all. Children of God practice righteousness, and they love their brothers. Loving and living—the two go hand in hand. John returns to those two ideas over and over.

John continues his exhortation to love:

Love One Another

1 John 3:11-15

¹¹This is the message that you heard from the beginning: we should love one another. ¹²Do not be like Cain, who belonged to the evil one and murdered his brother. And why did he murder him? It was because his deeds were evil and his brother's were righteous. ¹³Don't be surprised, brothers, if the world hates you. ¹⁴We know that we have passed from death to life, because we love our brothers. The one who does not love remains in death. ¹⁵Everyone who hates his brother is a murderer. You know that no murderer has eternal life abiding in him.

Cain's Negative Example

John returns to love as a mark of the person living in fellowship with God. Initially John told his readers that the commandment of Jesus to love was both an old commandment and a new one. There he contrasted love with hatred. Love gives direction to life. Here John emphasizes that loving was part of the initial message they received when they first learned the gospel. *The ethical demands on Christians do not change.*

John saw Cain as the perfect example of behavior that marks lost-ness. He was a son of the evil one and murdered his brother. John asks reasonable question: "Why did Cain slay his brother?" For John, the answer is obvious; Cain was jealous. His brother offered a sacrifice that was pleasing and acceptable to God. His sacrifice was not acceptable. He simply eliminated the competition.

73

We immediately ask, "Why wasn't Cain's sacrifice acceptable?" Some have said that God favored Abel's sacrifice over Cain's because Abel offered a *blood* sacrifice while Cain offered a *cereal* sacrifice. The problem with that theory is the first time a blood sacrifice was clearly commanded was after the flood. Moreover, grain sacrifice did play an important place the Old Testament sacrificial system.

Animosity toward brothers or sisters places those holding such hatred in the same category as murderers.

Others, following some of the church fathers, have suggested that Cain did not cut up his sacrifice the right way. There is nothing in the text to verify that.

Another suggestion is that Cain's sacrifice was unacceptable because Cain did not offer the best. The text says that Abel offered the fat of the firstlings of his flocks while Cain brought some of the fruit of the ground (Genesis 4:2b-5). Perhaps Cain brought the leftovers, not the best.

There is another possibility that seems best to explain the data. It seems that the problem was with Cain himself. The primary problem was not Cain's sacrifice, but Cain.

In Amos God said of Israel, "I hate . . . your religious feasts; I cannot stand your assemblies . . . . I will have no regard for [your offerings] . . . I will not listen to the music of your harps" (Amos 5:21-23). Why didn't God like their sacrifices? Did He not want them to give sacrifices and sing songs? Something was wrong with their attitude; they lacked justice, righteousness, and mercy (Amos 5:4-17, 24).

In Genesis 4, God said, "Cain, why is it that your countenance has fallen? Couldn't you change all of that if you wanted to?" (Genesis 4:6-7). The problem was Cain. That understanding fits well into the context of 1 John 3. The text says, "For what reason does he slay him? Because his deeds were evil and his brother's were righteous." Something was wrong about the way Cain was acting. Something was wrong with Cain the person. An early church father, Clement of Rome, contended that that was the reason for God's rejection of Cain's sacrifice. Cain had a bad attitude, a sinful disposition. That could account for Cain's faulty offering.

Cain went on to kill his brother because the sinful disposition led to an unacceptable sacrifice which in turn led to jealousy. John wanted his readers to realize what can happen when we hate our brother. Animosity toward brothers or sisters places those holding such hatred in the same category as murderers. Even though we may never murder our brother, when we do not take seriously our brother's life and when we do not seek our brother's good, we have the root attitude necessary to be a murderer.

Passing from Death to Life

We Christians should not be surprised when the world hates us. Cain didn't like his brother. He who is seeking God has something the world will never know—God's on his side. As a Christian some may give you a hard time because you make them feel uncomfortable. Your lifestyle will make them feel guilty.

"We know that we have passed from death into life because we have loved the brothers and sisters." Saying that you have "passed from death into life" is another way of saying that you are saved. How can you tell whether or not you are saved? Whether or not your life is headed the right direction? You must to examine how you treat brothers and sisters in Christ.

John is not talking about an emotional attachment but a lifestyle when he calls believers to love. It is putting fellow Christians first.

"The one who does not love abides in death. Everyone who hates his brother is a murderer. You know that no murderer has eternal life abiding in him." It would seem that John is echoing the words of Jesus: "Call your brother, 'racca'; call your brother, 'fool'; hate your brother; and you are guilty of murder" (Matthew 5:21-26). How I treat my brothers and sisters indicates the genuineness of my claim of fellowship with God.

An old Greek proverb says, "It is not what they profess but

what they practice that makes them good." We would say today, "Walk the walk not just talk the talk!" Practice does make the person.

PERSONAL INVENTORY

What direction is my life headed? Am I walking in the light?

Do I acknowledge the sin in my life and own up to my failures? Do I depend upon the saving blood of Christ?

Can I honestly characterize my life as obedient? Am I really striving to do God's will?

Do I live to help my brothers and sisters? Do I really love?

Where do things fall in my list of priorities? Does my relationship with God and spiritual things take precedence over the things the world would have me treasure?

Do I acknowledge Jesus as the Christ, the Son of God, in all that I say and do?

Do I abide in the apostolic teaching? Does the message of the Bible govern my life and my thoughts?

Do I let God work in my life? Do I search for His will or do I quench His Spirit?

Am I practicing sin or am I practicing righteousness?

LET'S GET PERSONAL

1. Christians today are not likely to fall prey to the Gnostic definition of sin as "not knowing the mystery." In what ways does John's teaching about "practicing sin" address the modern view of sin?

2. How does 1 John address the doctrine of "sinless perfection" or "the second work of grace"?

3. Give some examples of sin versus a sinful lifestyle.

4. Examine Genesis 4:2-5 and Amos 5:21-23 and list what made worship unacceptable to God in each passage.

5. Discuss how absence of love for brother, hatred for brother, and murdering brother are related.

Chapter 8
The Guilty Conscience
1 John 3:16-24

Greater love has no one than this,
that he lay down his life for his friends.
John 15:13

Most people have heard the story of the notorious boss who had a penchant for saving everything. Finally the files were bulging, and his poor secretary could take it no more. "We must dispose of the old useless stuff," she argued. At last her boss consented. But reluctantly he said, "We will destroy all those old files that we don't use, but be sure you make a copy of everything before you throw it away."

That is the way it is for many Christians with their guilt. Guilt just hangs on. Sincere people recognize only too clearly their shortcomings. How can I deal with a guilty conscience where the guilt is something I have laid before God but I cannot forgive myself and really wonder whether God can forgive me? For John the solution is tied to love.

Love Is Action

1 John 3:16-24

[16]This is the way that we know love: because He [Jesus] laid down His life on our behalf. And we ought to lay down our lives for our brothers. [17]Whoever has the stuff of life of the

world and sees his brother in need and shuts off his feeling from him, how can the love of God abide in him? [18]Little children, let us stop loving in word and in tongue. Let us rather love in deed and in truth. [19]It is by this that we will know that we are of the truth. And it is by this that we will set our heart at ease in His presence. [20]For if our heart condemns us, God is greater than our heart and He knows all things.

[21]Loved ones, if our heart does not condemn us, we have confidence toward God, [22]and whatever we ask we receive from Him, because we keep His commandments and do the things which are pleasing before Him. [23]And this is His commandment, that we should believe in the name of His Son Jesus Christ and should love one another just as He gave us a commandment. [24]The one who keeps His commandments abides in Him [God] and He [God] in him. And by this we know that He abides in us, by the Spirit whom He gave to us.

Measuring Love for Others

I know I am supposed to love my brothers and sisters, but just *how much* do I have to love them? Yes, love is putting them ahead of other things, but just what does that entail? Again John reminds his readers that Jesus is the paradigm for love. Telling God's people they should love their neighbors was not new. But when Jesus said, "Love as I have loved," that was new—that was radical. He laid down His life for us. That is what love is all about. John is not calling his readers to martyrdom, but he is calling them to a radical reordering of their lives—laying down their lives for brothers and sisters—putting their welfare ahead of personal desires. "We ought to lay down our lives for our brothers."

Laying down your life may sound glamorous. Besides, since that is not likely to be required of me, I can make a commitment to do it. But John does not let his readers off so easily. If you have the stuff that makes living possible,[24] see your brother in need, and "shut your bowels of compassion" (KJV), you do not have love and you are not demonstrating that quality you find in Jesus.

The phrase "bowels of compassion" in the *King James Version* is a very literal translation of the original. The Jews and the Greeks used a different system of body metaphors to convey abstract ideas than we would use today. For them, the intestines were the "seat" of feeling or emotion. I often tell my students that, had Jews of the first century sent Valentine's Day cards, they would have had a graphic representation of the lower GI tract rather than the heart. Today we talk about "gut-feeling" or "butterflies in our stomach." The heart in Jewish and Greek thought was the locale of the will or intention. When Jesus tells His followers that where a person's money is there will his or her heart be, He was informing them that the things they treasure will dictate their decisions.

A loving lifestyle is the clearest mark that you are really God's person.

When John refers to a believer who has the world's goods and does not take advantage of the opportunity to show compassion to a fellow Christian, he has simply picked an example of not laying down your life. It is interesting that John and James chose the same illustration to demonstrate love in word only and faith without deeds (James 2:15-17).

John has used three different words for "life" in chapter three. Christians "have passed from death to life" (3:14). That word for "life"[25] is John's word for *real* life, not just living, breathing, eating, and existing. It is usually accompanied by the adjective "eternal," life of the Christian age. In verse 16, John noted that Jesus "laid down His life for us." That reference of the word for life refers to Jesus' person.[26] The call is for Christians to lay down their very persons for their brothers and sisters. The third word for life[27] is translated "goods" or "stuff of life." How can we have *real life* and not lay down our *life* (our person)? If we lay down our life, we will share *the stuff of life.*

John asks, "How can the love of God abide in a man who doesn't share the things necessary for life?" Again we must decide whether "of God" is subjective or objective. That is, is John asking, "How can God's love for that man abide in the man?" Or is he asking, "How can that man's love for God abide in the man?" From the context it must clearly be the latter question that John has in mind. If you do not respond in love, a love that acts, toward a brother, do you really love God? Do you really appreciate what God has done for you?

John continues, "Little children, let us stop loving in word and in tongue. Let us rather love in deed and in truth." It is easy to claim you love someone, but demonstrating that is another matter. If "in word" and "in tongue" are a matched pair defining a single style of proposed "love," then logically "in deed" and "in truth" do the same thing. Love in deed is love in truth, real love.

How can Christians build their confidence regarding their relationship with God? "Love in action is how," John says, "we will know that we are of the truth. Love in action is how we will set our heart at ease before God." Sometimes I feel guilty—down on myself—uncomfortable about my relationship with God. How should I handle that feeling? John says, "Go out and do something loving for a brother or sister." *A loving lifestyle is the clearest mark that you are really God's person.*

Have you ever noticed how a loving deed does as much for the doer as the receiver? You feel better about yourself and your relationship with God. God loves, and we love in response. We share God's love.

By loving I assure my heart that I am really God's person. *The New English Bible* substitutes the word "conscience" for the word "heart" in verses 19-22. That seems to be the idea that John seeks to communicate. Conscience is vital for the Christian to function, but conscience can be wrong. I can be guilt ridden. I can proclaim myself a terrible, "unsaveable" person, someone who always fails God.

Building Confidence toward God

My heart, my conscience, is not the Holy Spirit speaking to me. Doing the loving thing will affect the conscience. But the conscience can still be wrong. Even when my heart continues to condemn me, God is greater than my heart and knows all things. He knows my struggle, my intentions, and my needs. If I strive to do the loving thing and rely on the saving blood of

Jesus—not my own feeble attempts at righteousness, God will have mercy on me. John's audience likely felt guilt and inadequacy even though they did not need to. They did not feel saved. Our study is entitled "Lord! Sometimes I Don't Feel Saved!" Once in a while, despite all of John's lessons to the contrary, Christians will feel that way. But if they can look at their lives and forge ahead to act out of love, they can count on God to take care of their needs. When I feel lost, I must do what I can, know that God understands, and rely on His grace.

Boldness rooted in the grace of God gives stamina in Christian living. It gives confidence in prayer. The Christian will have confidence to go to God knowing that whatever he asks from God he will receive because he keeps His commandments and does the things that are pleasing to Him.

All of those "whatever you ask of God . . ." passages can be a bit misleading. God has not given Christians a blank check, a little charge card for whatever we want with the bill sent to God. That is not what John meant when he told his readers, "Whatever we ask we receive from Him." Notice John narrows the "whatever" by describing the actions and attitudes of those who make the request: "because we keep His commandments and do the things that are pleasing before Him." There are some things that Christians do not ask for because they are learning what really matters.

Our prayers ought not to center on material possessions, things. When Jesus taught His disciples to pray (Matthew 6:9-13), He told them to pray, "Give this day our daily bread." The prayer was not "Lord, give us a villa on the Sea of Galilee" or "Lord, give us a fleet of fishing boats." Yet there is a real tendency for Christians to think that the appropriate prayer today would be, "Lord give me a Mercedes, and I will use it to your glory." Jesus taught that the appropriate prayer for the Christian was "Give me what I need to get through today, Lord." Unfortunately, our culture has confused necessities and luxuries.

Here John is telling his readers, and ultimately Christians of all ages, that God will supply their needs. He will take care of that persisting guilt. He will help Christians stand firm. They can approach God with confidence, stand before Him and tell Him what they need. "You know," John says, "that He won't withhold what you need. It will be yours. It will be provided for you."

Prayer helps me to gain a better sense of what really matters.

God does answer prayer. Prayer does alter the course of events. But *prayer also changes people.* Even if a Christian's prayer is materialistic, he needs to pray it. The Psalms are filled with the prayers of those whose attitude needed to be changed. What makes those prayers so important to the believer today is the fact that they are heartfelt prayers. When Jesus was in the Garden of Gethsemane, He prayed three times, "Let this cup pass from Me." He knew all along what His mission was, but He prayed what was on His heart. Out of that open discourse with the Father, He gained stamina and assurance for the mission. Prayer helps me to gain a better sense of what really matters.

Notice that John returns to one of the threads that runs throughout the book: obedience, doing what is pleasing to God. This time he gives a new slant to obedience by linking it to a two-pronged commandment: "that we should believe in the name of His Son Jesus Christ and should love one another just as He gave us a commandment." Those two prongs represent two more of the threads that run throughout the book: acknowledging Jesus and loving fellow believers.

Of particular importance is the simple phrase, "in the name of His Son, Jesus Christ." "In the name of Jesus" is a weighty concept. We talk about praying in Jesus' name, obeying in Jesus' name, and being baptized in the name of the Father, and of the Son, and of the Holy Spirit. There is a danger that the modern believer will begin to see some sort of magical formula being invoked with the "name of Jesus."

Praying in Jesus' name means praying by His authority and His person. The emphasis does not fall on what we say at the end of a prayer but in the realization of the One through whom the prayer has its validity. Jesus is my intercessor in prayer.

A name meant more for first century readers than what someone was called. That is why Old Testament characters had their names changed. Today people are typically named because (1) some ancestor had that name or (2) because someone liked the sound of the name. At the birth of a new baby, very few mothers and fathers say, "Let's find a name that has a meaning which will be descriptive of this child's character." Rather they say, "We like the sound of that first name and middle name together." Only later do they get around to checking the meaning of the name. Our middle daughter's name is Abigail, a very good Hebrew name. She might think we chose her name because of its meaning, "My father's joy." She is her father's joy, but we really picked the name because we liked the sound.

For Jews, a name stood for the whole person. Here John says the first fork of God's expectation is the command to "trust in the person of God's son Jesus Christ." Trust in who Jesus is, what Jesus did, and what Jesus is doing.

After referring to the second prong of that commandment— loving brothers and sisters as Jesus commanded—John goes on to say, "The one who keeps His commandments abides in Him [God] and He [God] in him. And by this we know that He abides in us, by the Spirit whom He gave to us." John returns to the work of the Holy Spirit in the life of the believer. Here again the danger of swinging from one extreme to the other comes in to play. One extreme would see the Holy Spirit whispering in the Christian's ear, telling him what to do. The other extreme makes the Holy Spirit almost the ink on the printed page, some impersonal force in the world, or maybe the member of the Trinity who wound up the church only to let her go on her own after the first century. The Holy Spirit is alive and well. He is at work in the Christian's life.

How does the Spirit work in the Christian's life? That I cannot explain. I see the Spirit's work in my life in retrospect. I know I am where I am in my Christian walk because of His influence in my life. The Spirit does not tell me something contrary to the written Word. But His influence is not limited to the written Word. I must be open to that influence. That is

Do I confidently take my requests before the throne of God? why Paul can say, "Now the fruit of the Spirit is love, joy, peace, patience, kindness, goodness, faithfulness, gentleness, and self-control . . . Since we live by the Spirit, let us walk by the Spirit" (Galatians 5:22-25). The Spirit is at work in the lives of Christians so that they might develop those characteristics that they could never really develop on their own.

How do I know that God is in me? Well, I look at my life to see whether I am really seeking His will. And I look for the influence of His Spirit in my life.

PERSONAL INVENTORY

What direction is my life headed? Am I walking in the light?

Do I acknowledge the sin in my life and own up to my failures? Do I depend upon the saving blood of Christ?

Can I honestly characterize my life as obedient? Am I really striving to do God's will?

Do I live to help my brothers and sisters? Do I really love?

Where do things fall in my list of priorities? Do my relationship with God and spiritual things take precedence over the things the world would have me treasure?

Do I acknowledge Jesus as the Christ, the Son of God, in all that I say and do?

Do I abide in the apostolic teaching? Does the message of the Bible govern my life and my thoughts?

Do I let God work in my life? Do I search for His will or do I quench His Spirit?

Am I practicing sin or am I practicing righteousness?

Am I working to help my brothers and my sisters to be what they ought to be? Am I "other-people centered" or "self-centered?" Do my decisions center around my wishes or do I really care about other folks?

Do I confidently take my requests before the throne of God?

Can I see the influence of God's Spirit in my life?

LET'S GET PERSONAL

1. Use a concordance to look up passages where the phrase "bowels of compassion" occurs in the KJV New Testament. Relate what you have learned in this lesson to those passages.

2. Use a concordance to look up passages where the "heart" occurs in the KJV New Testament. Relate what you have learned in this lesson to those passages.

3. What does 1 John teach regarding the Christian's view of "stuff"?

4. Why was it necessary for John to emphasize loving "in word" and "in deed"? Has anything changed in that regard today?

5. In what ways and with regard to what sins do Christians especially struggle with guilt wrongly felt? Why is this struggle so big? How can 1 John help in the struggle?

6. Evaluate the statement: "Prayer touches God, it will change you."

Chapter 9

How Can You Tell a False Teacher?

1 John 4:1-18

Can both fresh water and salt water flow from the same spring?
James 3:11

The bad guys don't always wear black hats. It is very difficult to sort out the good guys from the false teachers. Sometimes those false teachers are so smooth; they sound so smart; they seem to intend only good. How can you tell whether a man is from God or from the devil? John wants to give his readers some very clear clues.

John begins chapter 4 with, "Beloved, do not believe every spirit." The word "spirit" is John's link with the previous chapter. He has just told his readers that the Spirit, who has been given to believers, is a mark that God remains in them. A lot of people, including the false teachers of John's day, make the claim "We have the Spirit." How can we know whether someone really has the Spirit? The one who possesses the Spirit will teach the truth. How can we determine whether they are teaching the truth? The transition is quite natural.

The False Teacher

1 John 4:1-6

⁴:¹Beloved, stop believing every spirit, rather try the spirits to determine whether they are from God; because many false

prophets have gone out into the world. [2]By this you know the Spirit of God: every spirit that acknowledges that Jesus Christ has come in the flesh is from God, [3]and every spirit that does not thus acknowledge Jesus is not from God. This is the spirit of the antichrist, which you have heard is coming and is now already in the world.

[4]You are from God, little children, and you have overcome them because greater is the One who is in you than the one who is in the world. [5]They are from the world. On account of this, they speak from the world, and the world hears them. [6]We are from God. The one who knows God hears us. He who is not from God does not hear us. On account of this we know the spirit of truth and the spirit of error.

First Test for False Teachers

John gives two tests to help his readers determine whether someone has the Spirit or whether he or she is a false teacher. In John's day *one* test would clearly mark the false teacher. What do these people say about the incarnation, about Jesus coming in the flesh? The Docetics of John's day had no room for God coming in the flesh. These false teachers said, "Jesus wasn't God. Christ didn't come in the flesh. Christ adopted the man Jesus' body. Flesh is bad. God is good."

It is naive to think that the only question for determining orthodoxy today is, "Do you believe that Jesus is the Son of God who came in the flesh?" Saying yes to that question does not guarantee that a person is teaching the truth. That, however, is a vital question. If a person does not acknowledge that Jesus came in the flesh, he or she is a false teacher. It makes no difference what else he or she says or does. God's saving work in Jesus is the central doctrine of the Christian religion. Jesus came in the flesh; God was working in Jesus to save the world from sin. If you toss that out, the Christian religion is vain.

John again informs his readers that this false teacher is "the spirit of the antichrist." Notice that (1) John tells his readers what the antichrist teaches, and (2) he informs them that these antichrists have already arrived. The antichrist is not someone or something for which Christians today should be waiting with hopes for finding the time of the second coming.

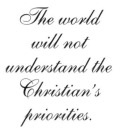

The world will not understand the Christian's priorities.

John reminds his readers that they are winners. They have overcome. If God is on their side, how can they be losers? The victory is theirs!

That victory is *ours* as well. We have overcome; we have won the battle. The fighting is not over yet; the devil is still at his old tricks. We have, though, already won because of what God has done and is doing in Jesus. False teachers talk like the world, and the world will listen to them. The world will not understand the Christian's priorities.

Second Test for False Teachers

John provides a *second* test for the false teacher: "We are from God. The one who knows God listens to us." Remember the key word for the false teachers? "We know God. We know the mystery." "If they don't pay any attention to us," John says, "then they don't know God." Who is the "us"? It is, undoubtedly, John and the rest of the apostles. False teachers will not listen to the message proclaimed by the apostles from the beginning. John has already indicated that one of the marks of the saved person is abiding in the apostolic teaching.

John's two marks of the false teacher are still valid. (1) What does the teacher say about the saving work of God in Jesus? (2) Does the teacher adhere to the apostolic message?

Back to Love

1 John 4:7-12

⁷Beloved, let us continue to love one another because love is from God and everyone who practices love has been begotten from God and knows God. ⁸The one who does not practice love has not known God because God is love. ⁹This is how

God made clear His love among[28] us: God has sent His one and only Son into the world in order that we might live through Him. [10]In this is love, not that we loved God, but that He loved us and sent His Son as a propitiation for our sins. [11]Beloved, if God loved us in that way, we ought to love one another. [12]No one has ever beheld God; but if we love one another, God remains in us, and His love reaches maturity in us.

An interesting exercise would be to underline every form of the word "know" each time it appears in 1 John. The word appears approximately forty times in 1 John. Because the false teachers kept saying, "I know," "we know," "we have special knowledge," John emphasized what Christians know: "you know," "we know." Everyone who practices love is born of God and knows God. Knowing God is what matters.

John provides a simple equation: GOD = LOVE. If God is love and someone does not know love, then how can he know God?

God loves us. But how do we really know that He loves us? God made it clear by sending His one and only Son. The Greek word translated "one and only" here[29] ("only begotten" in the *King James Version*) is a key word in the writings of John (cf., John 3:16).

Some have been troubled because recent translations have moved away from the translation "only begotten." They feel that in some way this move minimizes the virgin birth. The change in translation has nothing to do with the translator's position regarding the virgin birth. In reality "only begotten" owes its origin to the fifth century AD Latin translation by Jerome, the Vulgate.

The same word appears in Hebrews 11:17 where Isaac is called Abraham's *unique, one-of-a-kind* ("only begotten" in the KJV) son." Isaac was not the only son born to Abraham. Abraham had a son named Ishmael and other sons by Keturah his second wife. The man Isaac was described this way because he was unique, one of a kind. There were no others like him. It was through him that the promise of God was to be accomplished.

Similarly, at the beginning of the second century, Clement

of Rome used the same word in his letter to the Corinthian church to describe a phoenix bird, the legendary bird that rose from its ashes. Birds are not born; they are hatched. The phoenix bird was not even hatched. Clement used this word because that bird was unique, one-of-a-kind. There were no other birds like the phoenix bird.

We are sons and daughters of God, but Jesus' Sonship is different. God made His love very clear to us by giving His unique, one-of-a-kind Son. He gave Himself as a propitiation for our sins.

God Himself sent the sacrifice; He was the sacrifice; He was the place where that sacrifice was offered.

Do you remember the word "propitiation"? It appears only twice in the New Testament. In our discussion of 1 John 2:2, we learned that propitiation means something done to avert wrath. God has the right to be angry with me because of my sin, to be righteously indignant. But He sent His own Son to handle that wrath. God Himself sent the sacrifice; He was the sacrifice; He was the place where that sacrifice was offered (Romans 3:25). He did it all for me. That kind of love demands love in kind. If God so loved us, we ought to love one another. It is John's call for his readers to remember the parable of the unforgiving servant (Matthew 18:23-35). The debt we have been forgiven is so huge that, no matter what someone should do to us, that debt pales by comparison.

No one has ever seen God. We must, thus, measure knowing God in some other way. Loving one another is the mark of a person who has God abiding within. When we love one another, "his love is perfected in us" (KJV). The word "perfect" in the King James Version seldom, if ever, means "without error." It rather means complete, whole, mature, or reaching the intended goal. God's love reaches its goal when we respond with love. God loves me. When I love my brother, one of God's goals in loving me is accomplished and I move toward maturity.

91

More on the Indwelling Holy Spirit and Acknowledging Jesus

1 John 4:13-16

[13]By this we know that we abide in Him and He in us, because He has given us of His Spirit. [14]And we have beheld and give testimony that the Father has sent His Son to be the Savior of the world. [15]Whoever acknowledges that Jesus is the Son of God, God abides in him and he in God. [16]And we have known and have placed our trust in the love that God has for[30] us.

John returns to his argument that the indwelling Spirit is a mark of the one who is saved, that is, the one who abides in God (cf. 1 John 2:27; 3:24). Again the Christian is called to ask, "Is the Spirit working in my life? Is God working to help me mature? Am I developing the fruit of the Spirit? Am I becoming what God would have me to be?"

At this juncture John turns again to his call for Christians to acknowledge Jesus as the Son of God. John tells his readers that he and the other eye witnesses[31] are giving testimony to what they have seen—Jesus, the Son of God, the Savior of the World. The false teachers may try to separate Jesus and the Christ, but God will dwell only in the one who owns up in word and in deed to that fact that Jesus is the Christ.

When we acknowledge Jesus as the Son of God, we are claiming something more than a relationship arising from physical procreation. When Jesus is proclaimed "Son of God," He is declared to be someone who bears all the qualities of God. When we acknowledge that Jesus is the Son of God we proclaim Him to be *divine*—something the false teachers would never do.

We as Christians know God's love as displayed in Jesus. It is there that we have placed our trust. And why is that so? Because . . .

God Is Love

◄►

1 John 4:16b-18

[16b]God is love. The one who remains in love remains in God, and God remains in him. [17]In this love reaches maturity in us in order that we might have confidence in the day of judgment because just as He is, so are we in this world. [18]There is no fear in love. Mature love drives out fear because fear has to do with punishment. The one who fears has not become mature in love.

John returns to his equation *GOD = LOVE*. If we dwell in love, we dwell in God; if we dwell in God, we dwell in love. When we appreciate what God has done for us, we have to be loving.

"Perfect love" (KJV) or better "mature love" provides confidence for the believer. There is no room for fear in that kind of love. Fear is tied to worry about punishment. The word "fear" has two meanings in the Bible. When we read, "The fear of God is the beginning of all knowledge" (Proverbs 1:7), "fear" refers to reverence and awe. The other meaning is the "shaking-in-your-boots" kind of fear. Mature love does not do away with awe and reverence for God, but it does mean that the primary motivation for the Christian is not fear of punishment.

If we see God's love, understand His love, and allow that love to be reflected in our own lives, we will not approach Him shaking in our boots. Part of the problem is that Christians may view God as a "Cosmic Policeman." He practices entrapment to catch His poor creatures. We are spiders on the end of a web that God was dangling over the fires of hell (see chapter 2). But, that is not the kind of God we serve.

Fear does not serve as an effective "long-term motivation" (see chapter 3). Hell-fire-and-brimstone sermons wear off by Monday or Tuesday. But "the love of Christ constrains" always. God is not out to get us. He is on our side. That makes a difference in living the Christian life.

There are false teachers in the world, but Christians know what matters. God loves us.

PERSONAL INVENTORY

What direction is my life headed? Am I walking in the light?

Do I acknowledge the sin in my life and own up to my failures? Do I depend upon the saving blood of Christ?

Can I honestly characterize my life as obedient? Am I really striving to do God's will?

Do I live to help my brothers and sisters? Do I really love?

Where do things fall in my list of priorities? Does my relationship with God and spiritual things take precedence over the things the world would have me treasure?

Do I acknowledge Jesus as the Christ, the Son of God, in all that I say and do?

Do I abide in the apostolic teaching? Does the message of the Bible govern my life and my thoughts?

Do I let God work in my life? Do I search for His will or do I quench His Spirit?

Am I practicing sin or am I practicing righteousness?

Am I working to help my brothers and my sisters to be what they ought to be?

Am I "other-people centered" or "self-centered?" Do my decisions center around my wishes or do I really care about other folks?

Do I confidently take my requests before the throne of God?

Can I see the influence of God's Spirit in my life? Is my love for God and my response to Him maturing?

LET'S GET PERSONAL

1. Evaluate the two tests John gave his readers for locating false teachers in terms of their usefulness for the Christian today.

2. Examine the following passages where "only begotten" (monogenes) occurs in the Greek text of the New Testament. Determine which translation, "unique" or "one of a kind," fits each passage: Luke 7:12; 8:42; John 1:14, 18; 3:16, 18; Hebrews 11:17; 1 John 4:9.

3. Define mature love in terms of the way it would respond to God and to the world. Fill in the blanks with fear, habit, or love:

A. When I became a Christian, I was motivated primarily by _____.

B. Now my Christian walk grows out of _____.

4. Discuss the significance of the various answers to question 3 for living the Christian life.

5. Discuss how the church can help her members to develop a mature love.

Chapter 10

God Sits on the Witness Stand

1 John 4:19–5:12

For we cannot help speaking about
what we have seen and heard.
Acts 4:20

The prosecutor was browbeating the witness, and the judge would not step in. "How far were you from the front steps when you supposedly saw my client?" he asked. "Fourteen feet, seven inches," replied the witness. "How can you be so exact, pray tell?" "I knew some fool or other would ask me, so I measured it," replied the witness.

In the story above, we tend to have sympathy for the witness and might well believe him. But suppose the witness were God Himself. Surely we would be compelled to believe Him. In chapter 5, John will call God to the witness stand to defend the deity and manhood of Jesus. Before doing that John concludes his teaching about loving one's brother.

Loving One's Brother

◀▶

1 John 4:19–5:5

[19]We love because He [God] first loved us. [20]If anyone should say, "I love God," and practices hate[32] for his brother, he is a liar. The one who does not practice love for his brother, whom he has seen, is not able to practice love toward God,

97

whom he has not seen. [21]And this commandment we have from Him: the one who loves God loves his brother also.

[5:1]Everyone who believes that the Christ is Jesus has been begotten from God, and everyone who loves the begetter loves the one who has been begotten from Him. [2]By this we know that we love the children of God, whenever we practice love toward God and continue to keep His commandments. [3]For this is the love of God, that we continue to keep His commandments. Indeed His commandments are not burdensome [4]because everything begotten of God overcomes[33] the world. And this is the victory that overcomes the world, our faith. Who is the one who overcomes the world? Is it not the one who believes that Jesus is the Son of God?

Since God Loved First . . .

When the Christian loves God or loves others, it is not a work that earns him grand favor. God first loved us. You might say He invented love. In Romans 5, Paul argues that God loved us when we were "powerless" and "ungodly" (vs. 6), "sinners" (vs. 8), and "enemies" (vs. 10). We stood against God. We were not lovable, yet He loved us. He took the first step, and we love in response to His love—whether that love be for God or for brother.

Notice that John does not mince words: "If someone says he loves God, and hates his brother, he is a liar." John said earlier:

If we say we have no sin, we make God a liar (1:10). The one who claims to know God but does not obey His commandments is a liar (2:4). The one who denies that Jesus is the Christ is a liar (2:22).

There are witnesses who are not to be believed. It seems likely that the false teachers of 1 John had little concern for their brothers and sisters. John's call for love is a call for action.

It is easy for someone to *say*, "I love God." He does not meet God every day in a collision of personalities at work. She is not married to God. God does not take that last parking spot that I thought should have been mine. We can say we love God and not really have to demonstrate it because that love is abstract. Loving your brother or sister is another matter. John argues that loving God and loving fellow believers are inextricably bound. The way we demonstrate our love for God is by loving our brothers and sisters. That is God's commandment for living.

Loving God is also connected to what we believe about Jesus. If we believe that Jesus is the Christ, that indicates a new birth. That new birth indicates a new lifestyle, one characterized by love. Anyone who has this faith will love the God who acted in Jesus; that love will in turn cause him to love his brothers and sisters.

Begotten of God Means . . .

The "one begotten of him" in verse one could refer to Jesus. John would then be saying, "If you love God, you will love Jesus, His Son." From the context, however, the phrase refers to our fellow believer. The use of the word "children" in the second verse demands such an interpretation. John is not here arguing that anyone who contends that Jesus is the Christ is a Christian. Believing is not mere mental assent. It refers to putting our trust in Jesus as Messiah. With John's audience, that test was sufficient to delineate the false teacher from the true believer.

Believing is not mere mental assent. It refers to putting our trust in Jesus as Messiah.

That statement of faith is very important because it is the center for and foundation of the Christian faith. If we deny that fact, we are not part of the fellowship of believers because that fellowship rests upon the work of Jesus as Christ.

During the sixties and seventies, situation ethics became very popular. Its adherents claimed that there were no absolutes. Being ethical simply meant doing the loving thing in any circumstance. If something was done out of love, it could not be wrong; however, the loving thing is not always easy to determine. In fact, left to their own resources, human beings will often miss it.

If I love my brother, how will I know the loving thing?

John's answer is "Obey God." God's demands are not a bunch of dumb rules that say, "Jump this high!" "Jump this far!" They are not simply hurdles sent from God. Those commandments are designed to help man do the loving thing. Why does God say, "One woman and one man for life as husband and wife?"

Anything initiated by God cannot lose. Why does God tell His people what kind of workmen and bosses they are to be? Why all of those demands to be different from the world? God's commandments are not burdensome. They are designed to give God's people the fullest, best, and happiest life possible.

With both "overcomes" and "victory," John returned to the Greek athletic-shoe word, *Nike*, the shoe of champions. How can these Christians, indeed all Christians, know that they will win? Trust in the saving work of God in Jesus is the source of that victory. The only way we can overcome is by putting our trust in the fact that Jesus is the Son of God. Undoubtedly John's opponents looked like winners to the Christians of his day. The Christians felt like losers. John was reminding them of what *really* mattered.

Notice that John did not say, "*whoever* is born of God" but rather "*whatever* is born of God." Anything initiated by God cannot lose. The Christians' victory rests not in their own ability to accomplish great things but in what God has done and is doing in Jesus. "Who overcomes the world?" John asked. The victors are not the bad guys. The victors are those who place their trust in Jesus as the Christ. That is not a foolhardy thing to do, John argues, because God has given plenty of evidence. Now for the evidence:

Three Witnesses

1 John 5:6-12

⁶He is the One who came by water and blood, Jesus Christ. He did not come in water only, but in the water and in the blood. ⁷And it is the Spirit who testifies[34] because the Spirit is

the truth. [8]There are three that testify: the Spirit and the water and the blood. And the three are in agreement.

[9]If we accept the testimony of men, surely the testimony of God is greater because this is the testimony of God, which He has given concerning His Son. [10]The one who believes in the Son of God has the testimony within him. The one who does not believe God has made Him a liar because he has not believed the testimony that God has given concerning His Son. [11]And this is the testimony: God has given[35] us eternal life and this life is in His Son. [12]The one who has the Son has the life. The one who does not have the Son of God does not have the life.

The Three Witnesses Agree

What does John mean when he refers to Jesus as "the One who came by water and blood"? In the original language, one preposition ("by" or "through"[36]) governs the two objects "water" and "blood." The two words function as a unit.

John uses the metaphor of a law court with God calling the witnesses to the stand (5:5-8). According to Jewish law, for evidence to be acceptable, two or three witnesses were required (Deuteronomy 17:6; 19:15). God Himself provides three witnesses (5:8). If the witness of men is to be believed, surely we must accept the testimony of God.

There are a several options for understanding verse 6. (1) The passage may say that Jesus came with baptism and the Lord's Supper, and that these two ordinances bear witness to Him. Both baptism and the Lord's Supper point to the atoning work of Jesus; however, how would they serve as evidence of Jesus' deity and humanity? There is nothing in the context to indicate that John had this in mind.

(2) Perhaps John was reminding his readers of a passage that appears only in his Gospel. In John 19, the soldiers determined that Jesus was dead by piercing His side with a spear. Out of His body came blood and water. If that were John's purpose, he has reversed the word order. Also, what would this add to his argument? How do water and blood prove that

Jesus is the Christ, the Son of God, fully God and fully man?

(3) In verse 8 we find a clue to the meaning: "There are three that bear witness: the Spirit, and the water, and the blood." Somehow, water and blood, along with the Spirit, have to be evidence that Jesus is the Christ, the Messiah. Another clue is found in the nature of the false teaching that John has sought to refute throughout his letter. The false teachers claimed that Christ (God) adopted Jesus' body at His baptism and that He departed, leaving the man Jesus to suffer on the cross. "This is the one who came by water and blood." The same one who was baptized was the same one who died. At both events, God did something to indicate who Jesus was and is. At Jesus' baptism, God bore witness that Jesus was His Son; He spoke from heaven, "This is My beloved Son" (Luke 3:22). When Jesus hung on the cross, there was darkness, the veil in the temple was torn, and dead men were raised. These events declared, "This is a very special person who is dying on that cross, not just a man. He is God's Son." On both occasions, something unique happened.

At Jesus' baptism, it was Jesus Christ, not just a man adopted by God. On the cross, God's Son was dying. John's use of "water and blood" as a single unit indicates the entirety of Jesus' ministry. His whole ministry was a statement about who He was.

The third witness called to the stand is the Spirit. Throughout Jesus' ministry, the Holy Spirit bore witness to the fact that Jesus was the Messiah. It was the Spirit who gave Jesus the power to do the miracles. Jesus often said that the Spirit was working through Him (Matthew 12:28; Mark 1:10; Luke 2:27; 3:22; 4:1, 14, 18). When some of Jesus' opponents said that He was casting out demons by the power of Beelzebub, Jesus responded that they were blaspheming the Spirit, since it was the Spirit who was responsible for His ability to cast the demons out, not Beelzebub (Matthew 12:22-32; Mark 3:20-30; Luke 12:10-12).

The Spirit, John argues, is particularly qualified to bear witness because He is truth (cf., John 14:17; 15:26; 1 John 4:6). People may lie, but the Spirit will not.

God said something when Jesus was baptized, God showed something when Jesus died, and the Spirit gave evidence throughout Jesus' ministry. The three witnesses are in total agreement; Jesus is the Christ. The false teachers may try to deny it. They may think of some fanciful theory to explain it away, but they cannot.

God calls three witnesses to take the stand—the Spirit, the water, and the blood.

In the *King James Version* there is an additional sentence at verse 7. A second set of three witnesses appears. "There are three that bear record in heaven, the Father, the Word, and the Holy Ghost: and these three are one. And there are three that bear witness on the earth, the Spirit, and the water, and the blood: and these three agree in one." Why is the first sentence missing in most modern translations? That sentence is not found in the oldest Greek manuscripts of 1 John. The first Greek manuscript that has the sentence dates from the 15th century AD. The sentence has come to us from a sermon on 1 John by a Spanish heretic named Priscillian (d. AD 385). Priscillian added it in his sermon perhaps as an allegorical interpretation of the text. It then made its way into Latin translations of the New Testament. John's aim, at this juncture, is not to talk about the relationship between the Father, the Son, and the Spirit. In fact, the addition does not help John's case. His concern is for witnesses to confirm Jesus as the Messiah.

God calls three witnesses to take the stand—the Spirit, the water, and the blood. And the three agree. Notice that the witness, testimony, or evidence is in the believer. The witness is something that we should sense and feel. It is not *just* feeling, but it is a feeling.

God's Testimony Means Eternal Life

"The one who does not believe God has made Him a liar . . ." Why? Because God said, "This is My Son." He said it at His baptism, He said it at His transfiguration, He said it from the cross and in the resurrection, He said it in Jesus' teaching, and He said it in the miracles of Jesus. *If a person does not believe this, he calls God a liar!*

The consequence of the testimony that God has given is eternal life. God has given (past tense) believers eternal life. Again, eternal life for John is not length of life. It is *quality* of life. We begin to enjoy that life NOW! *Eternal life begins at the moment we accept Jesus as Savior, are buried in baptism, and become the new person.*

Life belongs to those who have the Son. We can claim to live without that relationship, but that is not really living. It is a relief when Christians finally realize that the victory rests, not in their own ability to accomplish great things, but in their trust in God, who has accomplished the victory through Jesus. That in no way minimizes the intensity we give to the Christian life, but it maximizes the security we enjoy in Christ.

Is there a witness within my life that Jesus is the Christ and that my victory rests in Him?

Sometimes I do not feel like a winner. I fail to live up to my own expectations for my life. I know I disappoint my God and others. In the world around me, the bad guy often seems to win. But, in Christ, I am victorious. In Him, my sins are washed away, my conscience cleansed, and my life transformed.

The external testimony that Jesus is God's Son and my Redeemer becomes an internal testimony (5:10). The message of the atonement transforms me. It is not just feeling, but it is a feeling. I begin to enjoy eternal life now. I have what really makes life matter. The culmination of eternal life is future, but that assurance of that final victory is a present reality.

PERSONAL INVENTORY

What direction is my life headed? Am I walking in the light?

Do I acknowledge the sin in my life and own up to my failures? Do I depend upon the saving blood of Christ?

Can I honestly characterize my life as obedient? Am I really striving to do God's will?

Do I live to help my brothers and sisters? Do I really love?

Where do things fall in my list of priorities? Does my relationship with God and spiritual things take precedence over the things the world would have me treasure?

Do I acknowledge Jesus as the Christ, the Son of God, in all that I say and do?

Do I abide in the apostolic teaching? Does the message of the Bible govern my life and my thoughts?

Do I let God work in my life? Do I search for His will or do I quench His Spirit?

Am I practicing sin or am I practicing righteousness?

Am I working to help my brothers and my sisters to be what they ought to be? Am I "other-people centered" or "self-centered?" Do my decisions center around my wishes or do I really care about other folks?

Do I confidently take my requests before the throne of God?

Can I see the influence of God's Spirit in my life? Is my love for God and my response to Him maturing?

Is there a witness within my life that Jesus is the Christ and that my victory rests in Him?

LET'S GET PERSONAL

1. Discuss the significance of John's statement: "God first loved us."

2. Compare the lyrics of the song "Faith is the Victory" with this lesson.

3. What makes the Christian feel like a loser in the world and in his life? How will John's message that Christians are winners affect the life of the Christian?

4. Evaluate the alternatives given for interpreting 1 John 5:6.

5. Why are the unique events that surround the baptism and the death of Jesus so important for John?

6. Compare John 10:10 and 1 John 5:11.

7. Evaluate the following statement: "While salvation does have a future component, it also has past and present components."

Chapter 11

The Crux of the Matter: The Cross

1 John 5:13-20

For the message of the cross is foolishness to those who are
perishing, but to us who are being saved it is the power of God.
1 Corinthians 1:18

crux [L cruc-, crux, cross, torture] 1 a: a puzzling or difficult
problem: unsolved question b: a determinative point at issue
2: a main or central feature

It is not unusual to hear someone proclaim, "The crux of the
matter is . . . ." Few people realize the connection between
that phrase and the cross of Jesus. What occurred there is "the
determinative point," the "main feature," and the "central
feature" of the Christian religion. In this section John will
again, although in an indirect way, emphasize the importance
of what God did in Jesus.

The Theme of 1 John

1 John 5:13-15

¹³These things I wrote to you who believe in the name of the
Son of God in order that you might know that you have eternal
life. ¹⁴And this is the confidence that we have toward Him: if
we should ask anything according to His will, He hears us.

15And, if we know that He hears us in whatever we ask, we know that we have what we have requested of Him.[37]

Confidence in Salvation through Jesus

The phrase "these things" does not refer only to the last section. John undoubtedly had in mind the whole letter. This has been the theme of the letter. This statement of purpose is a very natural transition from John's emphasis that *eternal life is to be found only in Jesus.*

Salvation rests upon the cross of Jesus and not on anything that I have done.

The *King James Version* has a different reading from the more recent translations at the end of verse thirteen: "These things I have written unto you that believe on the name of the Son of God; that ye may know that ye have eternal life and that ye may believe on the name of the Son of God." A few late manuscripts have this reading that probably resulted from a scribe remembering John 20:31 and then putting the two passages together.

Again, John uses a form of the word "know." Nearly forty times John has used or will use that noun or verb[38] to indicate that the false teachers do not know what is really worth knowing and that his readers do or should. The false teachers claimed to know the mystery. John tells his readers, "I want you to know this key thing: that you now have eternal life. It is your present possession."

We sometimes hesitate in saying, "Yes, I'm saved." Because we know our own sin, the ease with which we can turn our backs on God, and our own frailty, we are tempted to say, "I hope so" or "I'd like to think so" or "Maybe" or "If I don't fall . . . ." Some very religious people, who hold some very heretical positions, quickly answer the question with a resounding, "Yes!"

What is wrong? Why our lack of confidence? John's audience lacked Christian security because there were some things taking away that confidence. The false teachers probably made them feel inadequate. Their own failings made them feel inadequate. Our struggle is very similar. False teachers and personal failings produce some of the insecurity we feel. Also the over-reaction to "once-saved-always-saved" teaching has reinforced that insecurity. "Never-really-sure-I'm-saved" is not a happy way to live. Security was available for the Christian in John's day and is available to me today.

Salvation rests upon the cross of Jesus and not on anything that I have done. My trust is in Him. As long as that relationship is alive and well, I can say with certainty, "Yes, I am saved!" Christians should be able to look at those marks of the one who knows God, who is saved, and confirm that conviction.

Confidence in Prayer through Jesus

That security means confidence in prayer. "And this is the confidence . . . ." This is the fourth time that John has reminded his readers of the confidence they have in Jesus. The word for "confidence"[39] is literally, "freedom of speech." It is boldness to say what is on our heart, boldness to stand before a king and say whatever we wish.

Boldness in prayer is not a new topic for John (cf., 1 John 3:22). On both occasions when he discusses it, John links asking with the will of God: "keeping His commandments and doing the things pleasing to Him" (3:22); and "asking according to His will" (5:14). Again prayer is not free charge card for whims. Lifted out of context both passages have served as ammunition for "name-it-and-claim-it" theology. God is not offering the believer *carte blanche*. He balances the promise with an "if" phrase: "*if* we ask according to His will." Asking according to God's will is more than tacking "if it be your will" on the end of a prayer. It is a life-long search.

We must also understand what the will of God *really* is. Have you ever heard someone say, after a young child is killed in an automobile accident, "That was the will of God"? You might think that God wanted that accident to occur. The will of God is not a whim. The will of God often refers to God's plan, His sense of rightness. When Jesus prayed, "O my Father, if it is possible, let this cup pass from Me; nevertheless not My will, but Yours be done," He was bowing His desires to the grand scheme of God.

Praying *according to* *the will of God* *requires a* *searching* *heart.*

Praying according to the will of God requires a searching heart, searching for (1) the will of God in Scripture, (2) the maturity that comes from God in knowing what really matters, and (3) a zeal for the reign of God in your life.

Christians must have the conviction that, when they make a request from God, that request will be granted—in fact already has been granted—if it fits into God's plan and if their hearts are where the Lord's is. When we pray, "Lord, please heal Linda if it is your will" and Linda does not get well, we should not think that God wanted Linda to die. "Want" is not the issue. God has a plan, and for some reason Linda's healing did not fit into that plan which we cannot see or comprehend. God does intervene, and God does answer prayers; but He has set His own bounds. When Paul said, "All things work together for good to them that love God" (Romans 8:28), he was not saying that God causes every event. Certain things happen because of the "fallenness" of man. Every event will not be good. But God can and does cause good to come out of every event for Christians.

Unfortunately, our prayer often misses the will of God and centers on our will. It is easy to confuse wants and needs, the whims and the good.

The Sin Leading to Death

1 John 5:16-17

[16]If anyone sees his brother sinning a sin which does not lead to death, he will ask, and He [God] will give to him life for those who are not sinning sin which leads to death. Now there is sin that leads to death. I am not saying that he should ask concerning that sin. [17]All unrighteousness is sin, and there is a sin that does not lead to death.

Intercessory Prayer

The natural transition from prayer according to the will of God would include some discussion of intercessory prayer. We Christians who have the heart of God will care about our brothers and sisters. Their sins will hurt us because some will touch us personally. But they will also hurt us because we care. When a brother sins, Christians pray for him.

But John does not stop with the Christian praying for his brother or sister. He indicates a brother for whom this admonition does *not* apply: "one sinning a sin that leads to death." The words "lead" and "leads" are in italics because they have been supplied to help the sentence make sense in English. Literally the text says "a sin toward death." A similar phrase occurs in John 11:4. When Jesus receives news that His friend Lazarus was ill in Bethany, He told His disciples, "This illness is not unto death." Jesus was saying that the end result of Lazarus' illness was not to be his death. In 1 John 5:16, 17, John indicated that there is a sin whose end is death, spiritual death.

Just what is this "sin unto death"[40] which releases us from the obligation of praying for a brother? Some early church fathers thought this sin was something especially terrible, an unforgivable sin like murder or adultery. The background of the book is helpful in this regard.[41] The false teachers in John's day contended that Jesus was not the Christ, God's Son. He was a man whose body was adopted. From Him you could learn about enlightenment, but His primary task was not dealing with the human predicament because of sin. It seems logical that this teaching was the "sin unto death." Why? What is your outcome if you hold that position? It is ultimate spiritual death. There simply is no place to go if you turn your back on Jesus. God's work in Jesus is that central, key event in all history. The cross is the crux of the matter.

We can always pray for God to give us insight to help our brother change his mind about Jesus. But there is no forgiveness to be found until one comes to Jesus, the Christ, the Son of God.

Notice that this sin is not a single event or action. It is a stance, or attitude. *If a man turns his back on God's work in Jesus, there is no way for him to find forgiveness.* You can pray for him all you want, but there is only one place to find forgiveness, in the blood of Jesus.

Similar Passages

Two other passages carry a very similar idea. In Matthew 12:22-37,[42] "blasphemy of the Holy Spirit" is called the "unpardonable sin." Jesus had just performed a grand miracle. He had healed a demon-possessed man who was blind and mute. Everyone was amazed. The Pharisees were concerned and said, "This man casts out demons by Beelzebub, the ruler of the demons." Jesus responded, "It doesn't make sense for the devil to be fighting the devil. And if I, by Beelzebub, cast out demons, by whom do your sons cast them out?" Now He had them hooked. He continued, "If I cast out demons by the Spirit of God, then the kingdom of God has come upon you." The Spirit was working in Jesus (cf., 1 John 5:6). Jesus went on to say that a person could blaspheme the Son of Man and be forgiven, but if he blasphemed the Holy Spirit, he could not be forgiven. The Pharisees were practicing a defiant irreverence. They had evidence from the Spirit that Jesus was the Christ, the Son of God, yet they rejected Him. Jesus was not contending that the Son was less important than the Spirit. He was saying that if we reject the testimony of the Spirit about Jesus there is no place to find forgiveness. The sin was clearly not a single act; it was a stance.

The second parallel passage is in Hebrews 6:4-8. The author addresses Jewish Christians in danger of turning their backs on their faith in Jesus as Messiah. He argues that those who have enjoyed all of the blessings of the Christian faith and then continue to crucify Jesus by their lives cannot be brought back again to repentance. If we by our life reject or deny the work of God in Jesus, we have no place to turn and nothing to turn us around.

In 1 John the danger was people who denied the real person of Jesus. In Matthew it was those who did not see the Spirit at work in Jesus. In Hebrews it was those who would go back to an old system that made the work of God in Jesus insignificant. The crux of the matter is the cross.

The Christian Walk and God's Care

1 John 5:18-20

[18]We know that no one who has been begotten of God practices sin, but the one who was begotten of God keeps him and the evil one does not take hold of him. [19]We know that we are of God, and the whole world lies in the domain of the evil one. [20]And we know that the Son of God has come and has given us understanding that we might know the true one. And we are in the true one, in His Son Jesus Christ. He [Jesus] is the true God and eternal life.[43]

The sinful lifestyle is out of the question for us who are begotten of God. We will sin, but we cannot live a life of sin. We who are begotten of God are not left to our own resources because God keeps us. If God keeps, the devil cannot grab hold. The *King James Version* says, "the evil one cannot touch him." That translation may be a bit misleading. Does the devil ever touch you and your life? Of course he does. The word translated "touch" here also occurs in John 20:17 and 1 Corinthians 7:1. In John 20, Jesus instructed Mary Magdalene, "Do not touch me because I have not yet ascended into heaven." The danger was not that Jesus would disintegrate if Mary touched Him. The problem was that Mary wanted to hang on to Jesus and He was not back on earth to stay. In 1 Corinthians 7, Paul said, "It is good for a man not to touch a woman." Paul meant something more than a causal arm around the shoulder. Here John is arguing that the devil can never get a grasp on God's person. What a comforting thought! If the devil gets me, it will be my fault because God will do His best to keep me. And His best is very good!

John summarized the message of the letter for his readers, "It makes no difference what the false teachers know. Jesus came so that you might know—know the truth, know Him, know God. Now don't retreat from what you know."

Jesus is the Christ. He is the Son of God. He is God. He is eternal life. HE is the crux of the matter.

An Epilogue

1 John 5:21

Little children, guard yourselves from idols.

Have you ever read a book or seen a movie and been puzzled by the ending? At first reading we might have the same feeling about 1 John. "Guard yourselves from idols?" No "Good-bye"? No "Greet brother Demetrius"? No "Remember the point I have been driving home"?

Through 1 John there has been no mention of a problem with idolatry. In 1 Corinthians Paul had to warn the Christians about meat offered to idols, but there is no such warning in 1 John. Why then the admonition to guard themselves from idols?

Throughout the letter, John has reminded his readers of who they are in Christ Jesus and what they have in Him. He has continually warned them against a false teaching that would supplant God's saving truth which is to be found in the person and life of Jesus. That teaching or philosophy is an idol. The admonition is a very natural one: "Watch out for idols."

Our idols may not be a philosophy like Gnosticism, but they are real all the same. The "me-first" philosophy, the "grab-all-the-gusto-you-can-get" philosophy, the acquisition of stuff, the quest for power—these all supplant God and what He has done for us in Jesus.

Little children, guard yourselves from idols!

PERSONAL INVENTORY

What direction is my life headed? Am I walking in the light?

Do I acknowledge the sin in my life and own up to my failures? Do I depend upon the saving blood of Christ?

Can I honestly characterize my life as obedient? Am I really striving to do God's will?

Do I live to help my brothers and sisters? Do I really love?

Where do things fall in my list of priorities? Does my relationship with God and spiritual things take precedence over the things the world would have me treasure?

Do I acknowledge Jesus as the Christ, the Son of God, in all that I say and do?

Do I abide in the apostolic teaching? Does the message of the Bible govern my life and my thoughts?

Do I let God work in my life? Do I search for His will or do I quench His Spirit?

Am I practicing sin or am I practicing righteousness?

Am I working to help my brothers and my sisters to be what they ought to be? Am I "other-people centered" or "self-centered?" Do my decisions center around my wishes or

do I really care about other folks?

Do I confidently take my requests before the throne of God?

Can I see the influence of God's Spirit in my life?

Is my love for God and my response to Him maturing?

Is there a witness within my life that Jesus is the Christ and that my victory rests in him?

What is the CRUX of my life?

LET'S GET PERSONAL

1. Do you think John has succeeded in helping his readers to know they are saved? If so how?

2. William Barclay said, "We are apt to think that prayer is asking God for what we want, whereas true prayer is asking God for what he wants."[44] Evaluate his statement.

3. Discuss the significance of 1 John 5 for the Christian's prayer life.

4. Use a concordance to examine passages where the phrase "the will of God" occurs. What conclusions can you draw from these passages about the will of God?

5. Evaluate the following statement: "If you are worried about whether or not you have committed the unpardonable sin, stop worrying. You haven't."

6. Discuss the relationship between Christian security and the possibility of falling.

7. Considering 1 John 5, what do you think should be the basic message of sermons and Bible classes? How can this be accomplished?

Chapter 12

To a Special Lady

2 John

Many are called, but few are chosen [elect].
Matthew 22:14

What an interesting proclamation by Jesus! What was He telling His followers? That God would pick some and reject others according to His own desires and apart from their wishes? Hardly! This statement by Jesus follows the parable of the royal wedding feast (Matthew 22:1-13). Initially the invitation went out to the insiders, those who would be expected to receive an invitation to such a grand affair. They rejected the invitation with varying responses of disdain. Then the invitation went out to those folks from the wrong side of the tracks. Many of those people would come to the feast, be fitted with a wedding garment, and enjoy the celebration. One man, however, refused the garment and was rejected from the feast. Who then is called or invited? Well, ultimately everyone receives an invitation. Who are the chosen or elect? Are they not those who accepted the gracious invitation, not on any merit of their own, but simply those who said "yes"? They were those who chose to be chosen.

In Jesus' parable the fact that the individual's response is implied in no way denigrates the freely given gift, the invitation. In fact, the chosen or elect ones are still very special. They are desired; the host has planned for them.

John addressed his second letter to the "elect (or chosen)

117

lady," facing a situation very much like the one seen in 1 John. The bad guys in 2 John are the bad guys of 1 John. The followers of Jesus need to know that God wants them and cares for them.

The Prologue

2 John 1-3

[1]The elder,

To the chosen lady and her children, whom I love in truth, and not I alone but also all those who have come to know the truth, [2]on account of the truth which remains among (in) us. Indeed, it [the truth] will be with us forever.

[3]Grace, mercy and peace will be with us from God the Father and from Jesus Christ, the Son of the Father, in truth and love.

John calls himself "the elder."[45] Literally that term is a comparative adjective "older," used as a noun "older man." (1) The term can be used simply for those of advanced age. In many cultures, like that of John's own day, age demands respect. (2) Another option is to see the term used in the technical sense for those who serve in a leadership capacity in a local church. It would then be interchangeable with the term "bishop" or "overseer."[46] Since the apostle Peter refers to himself in such a fashion (1 Peter 5:1), and since John's work, according to tradition, was focused in one locale, this is indeed possible. (3) A final alternative is to see the term used as it will consistently be used in the second century, "those of old," "the ancient ones," "the eyewitnesses." No matter which way we understand the term, John's use of elder is his way of calling attention to his long connection with the church.

The phrase "the elect lady and her children" has long troubled those who read 2 John. Is the elect lady (1) some unknown sister in a local church; (2) a chosen woman name Cyria (making the word "lady" into a proper name); (3) a lady named Eclecte (taking "elect" or "chosen" as a proper name); or (4) simply a metaphor for the local church?

Although Clement of Alexandria, writing early in the third century, argued for option three above, it is very unlikely since we would need to assume two sisters with the same name (verse 13). Option two, identifying the sister as someone named Cyria, lacks early support. If we should choose to see the letter as written to an individual, option one is the best alternative.

We can, however, make a strong case for the term being a metaphor or personification of the local church. The pronouns for you[47] are plural (verses 10 and 12). The verbs are also generally plural (verses 6 and 8). While it is possible to see these plural forms addressing the lady *and* her children, this author prefers to see the figurative use of the term. Thus, "her children" would refer to members of the local church. Notice that the lady (the church) is chosen; she is special. By natural association so are her children.

While the key word in 1 John might be seen as "know" or perhaps "love," in 2 John it is "truth" which provides the focus. While it is possible to construe the phrase "in truth" adverbially as "truly," the frequent repetition of "truth" (verses 1, 2, 3, and 4) and the use of "deceives" and "false teaching" (verses 7, 9, and 10) make this unlikely. The truth is not here a philosophical term but undoubtedly refers to the gospel and its implications for the lives of believers.

John loves these people who are located in the truth because of their mutual concern for the truth. Grace and mercy and peace will be theirs because they are living out the truth and love, and are proclaiming truth and love.

Second John follows the normal pattern for a letter: author, audience, greeting, prayer/thanksgiving, body, farewell. John now moves to the body by way of a thanksgiving.

How We Live by The Truth

2 John 4-6

[4]I rejoiced greatly that I have found *some* from your children walking in the truth, just as we received a commandment from

the Father. [5]And now I ask you, lady, not as thought I am writing to you a new commandment, but *one* which we had from the beginning, that we should love one another. [6]And this is love that we walk according to His commandments. This is the commandment, just as you heard from the beginning, that we should walk in it.

Although the word "some" is not in verse four of the original, it is demanded by the structure of the language. It indicates that some of the children, the members, were no longer walking in the truth. John rejoices that "some," probably a majority, remain faithful to the message and its implications for their lives.

The call to adhere to the commandment to love one another is very much like what we saw in 1 John 2:7ff. (see chapter 4 of this book). On both occasions John notes that the command to love is not new. It goes back to the Law with its demand that one love his neighbor as himself (Leviticus 19:15). Indeed, the call to live a life of love does characterize the gospel and would be a part of what believers heard "from the beginning," that is, from their first experience with the gospel message. It is important to note that, for John, love is not simply something we do; it is a way to walk, a way to live.

Warnings against False Teachers

2 John 7-11

[7]Many deceivers who do not confess that Jesus Christ came in *the* flesh have gone out into the world; this one is the deceiver and the antichrist. [8]Watch out for yourselves in order that you might not lose the thing for which we have worked but *that* you may receive the full reward. [9]Everyone who goes beyond and does not abide in the teaching about Christ does not have God; the one who abides in the teaching, this one has both the Father and the Son. [10]If anyone come to you and does not bring this teaching, do not receive him into *the* house and

do not give him a greeting. [11]The one who gives him a greeting shares in his evil works.

John's compelling reason for writing about the truth and love is the rise of false teachers. The word for "deceivers" is a strong word which suggests "those who seduce" or "lead astray." These deceivers, like the false teachers of 1 John, are "antichrists." Their teaching is a denial that Jesus Christ came in the flesh (1 John 2:22f; 4:2, 15; 5:6f.).

John warns the lady and her children that they must watch out for themselves (note that the "you" here is plural). They must be careful not to buy into the message of the false teachers. Although in the New International Version John says, "Watch out for yourselves in order that you might not lose what you have worked for," the correct reading may well be "Watch our for yourselves that you might not lose what we have worked for." If this is so, John is concerned that his missionary effort might be to no avail and that his audience might lose the eternal life for which he and others have labored so hard.

The Christian life and Christian fellowship are based on the reception of the message of the incarnate Jesus.

If we do not abide (literally) in "the teaching (or doctrine) of Christ," we do not have God. Just what is this "doctrine of Christ?" There are two options: (1) a subjective option, "what Christ taught"; or (2) an objective option, "what was taught about Christ." In the context of 1 and 2 John, the problem is false teachers who deny that Jesus is the Christ and that He came in the flesh. It seems then that the second option, what was taught about Jesus, best fits the immediate context. What God had done and is doing in Jesus is the heart of the Bible. The Christian life and Christian fellowship are based on the reception of the message of the incarnate Jesus (John 1:1-18; 1 John 1:1-4).

Now suppose someone comes along changing that central teaching. How should the elect lady and her children respond to such a person? The word for "house" seems here to refer to the assembly. John is concerned that if the false teacher is treated as "a member-in-good-standing" or "an orthodox preacher," the message will be compromised and the witness of the lady and her children will be ruined. John warns, "Do not give him a greeting," literally, "Do not say to him 'Rejoice.'"[48]

Farewell

2 John 12, 13

[12]Although I have many things to *say* to you, I do not wish to write with paper and ink, but I hope to be with you and to speak *to you* face to face in order that our joy may be fulfilled.
[13]The children of your elect sister greet you.

We cannot be sure what other things John wished to say. Did he have in mind more harsh words for the false teachers or words of comfort and healing for the elect lady and her children? The latter seems more likely since he hopes to share those words "face to face" (literally "mouth to mouth") in order that our joy may be fulfilled."

John closes his letter with a customary farewell. He has used that plural "you" throughout the letter (verses 10, 12). He again picks up the metaphor begun in verse 1: "a lady and her children." If the lady of verse one refers to a congregation, then John is now saying that the congregation, of which he is likely a member, and its members, her children, send greetings.

PERSONAL INVENTORY
Am I known as one who knows the truth?

How do I recognize the truth living in me?

How am I assuring that I continue to walk in the truth?

Am I demonstrating God's love by keeping His commandments?

Have I unwittingly welcomed deceivers into my home?

Am I living my life fully expecting to receive my eternal reward?

LET'S GET PERSONAL

1. Discuss what it means to "walk in the truth."
2. How does John's admonition not to "greet" the false teacher have a bearing on the situation in a local church today?
3. Discuss the relationship between 1 and 2 John. What do they have in common?
4. Discuss the significance of being one of God's elect.

Chapter 13

To a Spiritually Healthy Man

3 John

*Do not forget to entertain strangers, for by so doing some
people have entertained angels without knowing it.*
Hebrews 13:2

There are several things about 3 John that make it unique. It is
the shortest book in the New Testament, the only book in the
New Testament not to mention Jesus or Christ, and the only
book by John to use the word church. Of all the books in the
New Testament, 3 John can best be described as a personal
letter.

Greetings to a Beloved Brother

3 John 1-4

¹The elder,
To the beloved Gaius, whom I love in truth.
²Beloved, I pray that in all ways you may prosper and be in
good health, just as your soul prospers. ³For I rejoiced when
the brothers came and bore witness of you in regard to the
truth, how you are walking in the truth. ⁴I have no greater joy
than this, to hear of my children walking in the truth.

Third John begins with the same opening as 2 John: "The
elder to _____, whom I love in truth." The emphasis

we saw in 2 John on love and truth is paralleled in 3 John.

The recipient of 3 John, "Gaius the beloved," should probably *not* be identified with any of the other New Testament characters who bear the same name (cf. Acts 19:29; 20:4; Romans 16:23; 1 Corinthians 1:14). Gaius was simply a very popular name in the Greco-Roman world of the first century.

A prayer that the recipient of a letter may experience good health was common in Hellenistic letters; however, John's request was a bit unique in one regard. Unfortunately, few Christians today would feel comfortable with John's prayer for Gaius: "May you be as healthy physically and in your business as you are spiritually." Many would rather that the prayer were reversed: "May you be as well off spiritually as you are physically and financially." John's expression of this hope is a compliment for Gaius. Gaius is a man with a good spiritual life.

Again John rejoices that a brother is walking in the truth (cf. 2 John 4). Brothers, perhaps visiting missionaries, have been coming to John and reporting about Gaius and his life. Throughout 3 John these traveling brothers play an important role. Although the connection between the false teaching in 1 and 2 John with the situation in 3 John is unclear, these "brothers" undoubtedly carry the true teaching about Jesus.

The primary concern in 3 John is not doctrine, that is, theological teaching, but rather lifestyle and love for and hospitality toward "the brothers." John's greatest joy came when he saw his children, those whom he had taught, walking in the truth (cf. 2 John 4).

Praise for Gaius' Hospitality

3 John 5-8

⁵Beloved, you are acting faithfully in whatever you do for the brothers, and this is *especially so when they are strangers*. ⁶*These are* those who bore witness to your love before the church, with regard to whom you do well when you send them forward in a manner worthy of God. ⁷For they went out for the

sake of the Name, accepting nothing from the Gentiles. [8]Therefore we ought to entertain such men in order that we might become coworkers with the truth.

John continues his praise for Gaius by emphasizing the faithfulness of his behavior toward the brothers, especially the strangers. The picture we should see is that of traveling missionaries who come from John to Gaius' hometown. These missionaries were to go on their way to other regions preaching the gospel. John is simply encouraging Gaius to continue to demonstrate hospitality for these workers.

When a person showed hospitality, as Gaius, he became a coworker in or with the truth.

Gaius' actions demonstrate a life "worthy of God." If we strive to live a life worthy of God, the gospel, and one's calling (cf. Philippians 1:27; Colossians 1:10; 1 Thessalonians 2:12), we will be the kind of persons who will glorify God, grow in His faith, and be happy Christians. Gaius' life was worthy of God because these missionaries had gone out for the sake of *the Name*. The phrase "the Name" is John's magnificent description of the cause of Christ, the reign of God, the church.

These itinerant missionaries did not receive anything from the "Gentiles." In 3 John all the names are "Gentile" (that is, non-Jewish) names: Gaius, Diotrephes, and Demetrius. John is using the term to refer to unbelievers. He thus means pagans or "the world." Taking nothing from unbelievers meant that the missionaries were totally dependent upon the brothers and sisters like Gaius. Without their hospitality, the missionary efforts of the church would grind to a halt.

When a person showed hospitality, as Gaius, he became a coworker in or with the truth. Although Gaius was not a traveling missionary, he was doing mission work all the same. The word translated "entertain"[49] in verse 8 is rendered "receive" by the *King James Version* but on the basis of usage by contemporary writers likely signifies "support" in the present context.

Note the contrast between the hospitality for which Gaius

is commended in 3 John and the hospitality which "the elect sister" is told to withhold from the itinerant teachers John describes as deceivers and antichrists in 2 John. Just as receiving a proclaimer of the truth allowed you to participate in the proclamation of the truth, receiving a deceiver made you a party to his deceit.

Diotrephes

3 John 9-10

[9]I wrote something to the church, but Diotrephes, who loves to be first among them, does not receive us. [10]On account of this, if I come, I will remember his works which he does, unjustly accusing us with evil words. And not being satisfied with this, he does not receive the brothers and prevents those *who wish to do so* and puts *them* out of the church.

Apparently John had written to the church in the region where Gaius lived instructing them regarding the need for hospitality for the traveling missionaries. Diotrephes is apparently functioning in some sort of leadership position in either the congregation where Gaius worships or perhaps in a neighboring "house church." It is impossible to tell from the context whether Diotrephes differs theologically with the missionaries sent out by John or simply is jealous of John's exerting influence over the church where he served. Whatever the case, John tells us that Diotrephes "loves to be first among them" or as the KJV puts it "he loveth the pre-eminence." It is very easy to see the danger of power that turns the head of a "good man." Service can easily take second place to position and authority.

John promises that if he makes a visit he will deal with Diotrephes face to face. Diotrephes is talking nonsense about John and the brothers and brings unjustified charges against them. He refuses to accept the visiting missionaries and show them hospitality, and, if that were not bad enough, he makes welcoming and sharing with these brothers grounds for being excluded from the fellowship of the church. Diotrephes is trying "a power move" both to demonstrate and maintain his authority.

Demetrius and the Good

━━━━━━━━━━━━━━◄●►━━━━━━━━━━━━━━

3 John 11-12

[11]Beloved, do not imitate the bad but the good. The one who practices good deeds is from God. The one who practices evil has not seen God. [12]Demetrius has been borne witness to by all and by the truth itself. And we bear witness of him ourselves, and you know that our testimony is true.

John's admonition to imitate the good and not the bad looks back to the uncharitable behavior of Diotrephes in verses 9-10 and head to the commendable character of Demetrius. The actions of a Diotrephes were detrimental to Christian fellowship and the advance of the Name. He who practices good (notice John's call again for a lifestyle) is "of God" (cf. 1 John 3:10; 4:4, 6; 5:19). Doing the good grows out of our relationship with God. The Christian must behave that way. He who practices evil, that is, lives a wicked life, has not seen God (cf. 1 John 3:6; John 14:9).

Doing the good grows out of our relationship with God. The Christian must behave that way.

John commends by name Demetrius, one who practices the good. We know nothing of Demetrius outside this letter. The natural inference from the context would be that Demetrius was one of the traveling missionaries and was perhaps even the bearer of this letter. He may well have been John's special emissary to the city bringing special news and instructions. Diotrephes would thus be hostile to him, and he would need the support of Gaius.

John will follow a pattern we have already seen in 1 John 5:7-8 and call three witnesses to the stand (cf. Deuteronomy 17:6; 19:15; Matthew 18:16). This time the witnesses will testify to the character of Demetrius. First, Demetrius has a reputation among the churches where he is known. They could all testify as to his character. Secondly, the truth itself serves as a witness. It would seem likely that what he means here coincides with John's use of the term elsewhere (1 John 1:6; 2 John 4; 3 John 3). When you square the life and teaching of Demetrius with the gospel, the good news of the work of God in Jesus, his good character becomes evident. The third witness is John himself. John's own position, character, and reputation were well known and accepted by Gaius.

The Conclusion

3 John 13-15

> [13]I had many things to write to you, I do not wish to write to you with ink and pen. [14]But I hope to see you soon and we will speak face to face. [15]Peace be to you. The friends greet you. Greet the friends by name.

The closing verses of 3 John parallel the ending of 2 John. Again John indicates he has many things to say but would prefer not to put them on paper. Instead he wants to speak with Gaius face to face.

John then conveys greetings from common friends to Gaius and asks Gaius to greet mutual friends in his locale. Friends here seems to convey something more than common acquaintances; these are "brothers and sisters," "beloved ones." Even the note "greet . . . by name" indicates something of the closeness of the relationship. The pronouncement of peace follows the normal Jewish and early Christian custom for greetings and farewells—SHALOM. It may well call to mind Jesus' promise to leave His peace with His followers (cf. John 14:27; 16:33; 20:19, 21, 26).

In 2 John, John warned a sister church to guard the truth, especially the truth that Jesus came in the flesh. There were traveling deceivers who would come to the church spreading such false teaching. Third John, on the other hand, is an appeal for continued support for faithful brothers traveling to spread the gospel. John warns about Diotrephes who hinders the work of these good brothers. The contrast between how we are to respond to the teachers of truth and how we are to respond to the deceivers is very clear.

PERSONAL INVENTORY

Do I pray for both the spiritual and physical health of others?

Am I known for my faithfulness?

Would someone write home about my Christian life?

How would I be known for my love?

Do I enjoy giving money to missionaries?

Am I known for my hospitality?

What safeguards to I have in my life to keep me from imitating evil?

Would my life be characterized by my doing good or doing evil?

LET'S GET PERSONAL

1. Discuss the significance of "walking in the truth" and "walking in love."

2. Discuss how you might "love to be first" like Diotrephes and what this would mean in terms of the functioning of a local church.

3. What admirable qualities can you find for Gaius? What are the admirable qualities you see for Demetrius?

4. Someone has said, "Hospitality is a lost art." Respond to that statement. What is the significance of 3 John in this regard?

5. What are the implications of 3 John for the participation of members of a local church in the work of missionaries? How can a local church help members feel a part of the mission effort?

Conclusion:

Our Confidence in Christ

And surely I am with you always, to the very end of the age.
Matthew 28:20

What, then, shall we say in response to this? If God is for us, who can be against us? He who did not spare his own Son, but gave him up for us all—how will he not also, along with him, graciously give us all things? Who will bring any charge against those whom God has chosen? It is God who justifies. Who is he that condemns? Christ Jesus, who died—more than that, who was raised to life—is at the right hand of God and is also interceding for us. Who shall separate us from the love of Christ? Shall trouble or hardship or persecution or famine or nakedness or danger or sword? . . . No, in all these things we are more than conquerors through him who loved us. For I am convinced that neither death nor life, neither angels nor demons, neither the present nor the future, nor any powers, neither height nor depth, nor anything else in all creation, will be able to separate us from the love of God that is in Christ Jesus our Lord (Romans 8:31-39).

The pendulum is always swinging. May we land securely between the two extremes (once-saved-always-saved and never-really-sure-you're-saved) and proclaim, "I am saved." Our security rests solely on the saving work of God in Jesus our Messiah, our Savior, and our Lord.

We can find security by examining our lives to see God's

133

work. What really matters is our lifestyle. That lifestyle should be characterized by obedience, love, acknowledgement of our sins, and trust in our God.

The aging apostle John wrote to struggling Christians in the first century. We have had the privilege of reading their mail. As we have learned what John intended to teach them, we now make application of his message to our lives. If John had a pen and paper to write letters to us today, his message might vary little. He would still say, "My little children, know that you're saved, love one another, live lives that bring glory to God, and keep yourselves from idols!"

May we learn to move from "But Lord, sometimes I don't feel saved" to "Lord, I know I'm yours; I'm saved and I praise you for it."

Notes

Chapter One

1. Greek, *gnōsis* (γνῶσις)
2. Greek, *dokeō* (δωκέω)

Chapter Two

3. The translation of John's letters throughout this book is the author's own translation.
4. Greek, *koinōnia* (κοινωνία)
5. Greek, *hamartanō* (ἁμαρτάνω)
6. Greek, *homologeō* (ὁμολογέω)

Chapter Three

7. The Greek word is *paraclētos* (παρακλήτος, cf. our word "paraclete"). The *King James Version* translates this word as "Comforter." The root meaning of this word is "one called alongside to help." The term is used in law to refer to an attorney. The *New International Version* renders it as "Counselor," while the *New American Standard Bible* chose "Helper."
8. A Greek present participle
9. That phrase is ambiguous in most English translations as it was in the Greek in which John wrote. When Greek scholars discuss the phrase, they describe it as either subjective or objective. They are trying to decide from the context whether John is talking about God as the one who loves or the one who is loved.

Chapter Four

10. Donald E. Wildmon, *Thoughts Worth Thinking* (Tupelo, MS: Five Star Publishers, 1968), p. 101.

11. There are at least four words for love in Greek: *agapaō* (ἀγαπάω, ἀγάπη), eros (ἔρος), storgē (στόργη), and phileo (φιλέω).
12. The word *agapaō*, the verb form of *agapē* is not always used in a positive light in the New Testament (cf. 2 Peter 2:15; 1 John 2:15). In such passages *agapaō* still carries the idea of setting one person, thing, or goal ahead of another.
13. Greek, *agapaō* (ἀγαπάω)
14. The word translated "him" here can be either neuter or masculine. If taken as neuter, the word refers to "the light"; and the verse would be rendered: "the one who loves his brother abides in the light, and there is no cause for stumbling in it (the light)." If it is masculine (the assumption of this author), then the word refers either to the brother who does the loving or to the brother who is loved.

Chapter Five
15. Greek noun *nikē* (νίκη) and the Greek verb *nikaō* (νικάω)
16. This time John uses a different word for "children" than the word he used in the first stanza.
17. The noun *epithumia* (ἐπιθυμία) and the verb *epithumeō* (ἐπιθυμέω)
18. The *New International Version* has translated the phrase: "pride in possessions." The lexicon of Bauer-Arndt-Gingrich suggests "pride in one's possessions." The term refers to the search for status, the desire to be important.

Chapter Six
19. Greek, *antichristos* (ἀντιχρίστος)
20. Greek, *chrisma* (χρίσμα)
21. Greek, *christos* (Χρίστος)
22. Greek, *homologeō* (ὁμολογέω); cf. 1 John 1:9
23. Or "*when it is made clear*"

Chapter Eight
24. There are two Greek words for life. One (*zōē*, ζωή) is the word John uses with the adjective "eternal" to talk about real life which is found in Jesus. The Greek word here (*bios*, βίος) is used of the things necessary for physical existence.

25. From this word (*zōē*, ζωή) we get zoology.
26. The word here is *psuchē* (ψύχη), the word from which we get psychology. It is normally translated "soul." This word also appears in 1 Peter 3:20 that describes the ark as a vessel in which "eight souls" (NIV "people") were saved.
27. This word (*bios*, βίος) is the one from which we get biology. It refers to the "stuff" necessary for life. It is used in Mark 12:44 where the widow who put in two mites is described as putting in "all she owned, all she had to live on (literally, 'all her life')."

Chapter Nine
28. The Greek word *en* (ἐν) can be translated either "in" or "among."
29. Greek, *Monogenēs* (μονογενής)
30. Literally, "in" or "among"
31. Notice the subtle change in the meaning of "we." In 4:4-13, "we" refers to all Christians. Now "we" refers to the apostles and other eyewitnesses "who have beheld."

Chapter Ten
32. The tense of the Greek verb here indicates a practice of hating (present tense in Greek) versus a simple statement of fact (the aorist tense in Greek). Similarly, loving brother and loving God at the end of this verse indicate a practice.
33. Or "is victorious over"; cf. the next two occurrences of "over comes"
34. Or "bears witness"; "gives evidence"
35. Literally, "which God has testified"
36. In Greek, *dia* (δία)

Chapter Eleven
37. Literally, "we know that we have the requests which we requested from him."
38. "Know" and "knowledge" are represented by the Greek words *ginōskō* (γινώσκω), *oida* (οἶδα), and *gnōsis* (γνῶσις).
39. Greek, *parrēsia* (παρρησία)
40. The *Revised Standard Version* translates this phrase "mortal sin."
41. Some want to see "the sin leading to death" as unconfessed sin. While this position is attractive in light of 1 John 1:9, there seems to be more at work here. The position that the sin

is an unacknowledged one is not inconsistent with the position discussed here. If one does not believe the right thing about Jesus and what he did to handle our sins, he will never acknowledge his sins.

42. Cf. Mark 3:20-30; Luke 12:8-10

43. The language of verse 20 is difficult. It could mean the following:

    (1) "The true one" and "the true God" both refer to God the Father.

    (2) "The true one" and "the true God" both refer to Jesus.

    (3) "The true one" refers to God the Father, but John goes on to confirm that Jesus is "the true God and eternal life."

    Options 2 and 3 seem to be the most likely. See 1 John 5:11 where Jesus is clearly identified with "eternal life."

44. William Barclay, *The Letters of John and Jude*, Daily Study Bible (Edinburgh: St. Andrews Press, 1958), p. 137.

Chapter Twelve

45. Greek, *presbuteros* (πρεσβύτερος)

46. Greek, *episkopos* (ἐπίσκοπος); cf. Acts 20:17,28; Titus 1:5,7

47. Greek, *humas* (ὑμας), and *humin* (ὑμιν)

48. Greek, *chairein* (χαίρειν)

Chapter Thirteen

49. Greek, *apolambanō* (ἀπολαμβάνω)

Suggested Reading List

Akin, Daniel L. *1, 2, 3 John* (The American Commentary: An Exegetical and Theological Exposition of Holy Scripture). Nashville: Broadman, 2001.

Burge, Gary M. *The Letters of John* (The NIV Application Commentary). Grand Rapids: Zondervan, 1996.

Kistemaker, Simon J. *James and I-III John*. Grand Rapids: Baker, 1986.

Kruse, Colin G. *The Letters of John* (The Pillar New Testament Commentary). Grand Rapids: Eerdmans, 2000.

Roberts, J.W. *The Letters of John* (Living Word Commentary). Austin: Sweet, 1968.

Smith, D. Moody. *First, Second, and Third John* (Interpretation: A Bible Commentary for Teaching and Preaching). Louisville: John Knox Press, 1991.

Womack, Morris. *1, 2, 3 John* (College Press NIV Commentary). Joplin: College Press, 2000.